Frameworks

STRIVERS - NOT QUESTIONING
" DISCRIMINATING

CHALLENGERS NOT SOBER
" CAUTIOUS
SEEM TO BE UNNECESSARY
EVEN DANGEROUS

Frameworks

PATTERNS OF LIVING AND BELIEVING TODAY

Douglas Alan Walrath

THE PILGRIM PRESS
NEW YORK

Library of Congress Cataloging-in-Publication Data

Walrath, Douglas Alan, 1933–
Frameworks : patterns of living and believing today.

Bibliography: p. 103.
1. United States—Religion—1960–
2. United States—Social conditions—1980–
I. Title.
BL2525.W37 1987 277.3′0828 86-25407
ISBN 0-8298-0743-8 (pbk.)

The Pilgrim Press, 132 West 31 Street, New York, New York 10001

For my mother and father

Contents

List of Tables and Illustrations

SHAPING CULTURE
REFLECTING CULTURE

Preface

In 1965 I concluded a seven-year pastorate with a small, village church and became the senior minister of a large, suburban congregation. I sincerely tried to serve the new congregation with the same effectiveness as I had enjoyed in the village church. But I never felt satisfied with my ministry in the suburban church.

As a pastor in the rural community my role was well defined and broad; in the fast-paced suburb it was amorphous and constricted. The church in the small town was interconnected with all of life; the church in the suburb was contained and isolated. When I moved to the village in the late 1950s, nearly everything I had been taught in seminary about ministering worked well. In the new church I found that neither my experience nor my education had adequately equipped me for ministry. I faltered.

Within a year I did what I have learned many ministers do when they don't know how to cope: I went back to school. Taking to heart some advice from a respected, seminary sage ("For heaven's sake, don't study more theology; you already know how to do that!"), I began graduate study in sociology and social research. My goal was to discover why social change was challenging familiar roads to faith and the church, as well as the patterns of ministry for which I was prepared. I did not realize then that I was embarking on a journey of research and reflection that would stretch over the next twenty years.

In 1968 I responded to an invitation to serve as a synod executive. A decade of being responsible for more than one hundred churches and pastors widened my perspectives, as have several more years of working throughout the United States and Canada as an independent church-strategy consultant. These broader contexts afforded countless opportunities to see firsthand the many ways social change in this century has undermined traditional roads to faith and the church.

Forged as they were by such varied experiences, the personal perspectives through which I view social change and the church give strength to this book. Those experiences probably also define its limits. I have always lived and ministered within what is popularly known as the "mainstream" church. Mainstream denominations are generally seen as reflecting, as much as shaping, mainstream American culture. This church of the center is the church within which I was nurtured and for which I was trained to be a minister. Admittedly, many people and congregations are beyond the confines of the mainstream church. Only occasionally do they fall within the focus of this book. My lack of attention to them should not be construed as a value judgment; I am simply not equipped, in terms of either personal or professional experience, to discuss them adequately.

Another conscious limitation is theological. I have endeavored *not* to write from a particular theological perspective—at least not prescriptively. I have tried to describe some of the frameworks within which I think people *do* and *can* approach believing and the church today. The theological aspect of my approach is thus more operational than doctrinal. Throughout most of the book I am more concerned to describe the perspectives (theological and otherwise) with which people begin than to suggest how they should change them.

Especially in the last chapter, however, it becomes apparent that I am an incurable pastor. I do want people to find faith that is both theologically sound and helpful to them. I have devoted the bulk of the book to describing where people are now "coming from" because I believe that such understanding is an essential first step in sharing faith. In the face of the cultural pluralism that now marks society, I think that all of us who care about helping others to become Christian believers need to take seriously those who proceed toward faith within frameworks that are different from ours. At certain points in the book most readers who are Christians *and* church members will find themselves saying, "That certainly doesn't seem necessary to me." To which I respond, "What you are calling 'unnecessary' may be essential to someone else's faith development." Usually we can best help people to grow in faith when we accept where *they* begin, and suggest patterns of faith development that we have learned are possible for people like them.

The most serious failing that afflicts those of us who want to share Christian faith is our tendency to talk before we listen, to assume we know the answers before we hear someone's questions. We then batter other people with suggestions about believing that are not helpful to them. I hope this book helps others to appreciate, as I have, how difficult it is for many of those who now compose American society to approach believing in the ways in which many of us who are already church members think they ought to. More often than not today, I think we need to listen intently to others before we can make suggestions about believing that they will find genuinely helpful.

When Marion Meyer, my editor at The Pilgrim Press, read the original manuscript, she suggested several points of clarification. One of these, the preponderance of males in the illustrative material in the first half of the book, requires some explanation. The majority of males in some sections of these chapters reflects my experience in the church in the fifties, sixties, and even the early seventies. I feel considerable discomfort with that experience from the vantage point of the present, but during those earlier years, especially in more conservative denominations like my own (Reformed

Church in America), the leaders in nearly all congregations were males. Although I regret the sexist attitudes most of us took for granted in those years, in point of fact most of the leaders with whom I worked were men. Thus, when I describe what happened, most of the actors in the narrative are men. Along with most of my female and male colleagues today, I am grateful that those years of male dominance are past—and that we all benefit from the unique insights and contributions of the many women who now also lead the way in the Christian church.

Many people have contributed to the development of this book. I am grateful to all of them, but I would be remiss if I did not mention by name a few who have been especially helpful.

Nearly ten years ago, with the support of Robert Lynn, the Lilly Endowment provided funds that enabled me to gather together and interpret my research over the previous decade. I continue to benefit from the thinking I was able to do during those months. On several occasions I have talked my work through with my friend Carl Dudley and enjoyed the benefit of his critical comments. President G. Wayne Glick and Marvin Ellison, my colleagues at Bangor Seminary, read portions of the manuscript and offered helpful suggestions. Marion Meyer, senior editor at The Pilgrim Press, has supported me faithfully through a project that stretched over more time than either of us anticipated in the beginning. In the pages ahead my wife, Sherry, will recognize how many perceptive insights she has contributed. During years of thinking and seemingly endless rewriting she has given me her steadfast support.

Douglas Alan Walrath
Strong, Maine

DOCTRINAL
OPERATIONAL

SOUND - CREDIBILITY THEORY
HELPFUL PLAUSIBILITY PRACTICE

EARS HEART - LISTENING
EYES - HANDS - TALKING

Frameworks

CHAPTER ONE

Perspectives

The world we humans see is of our own making—although most of us seldom realize that we are constructing our own reality. Even many of the wisest among us assume a simple process of interaction: through our senses we relate to the world and experience directly what is there. We "reach out and touch" the world around us.

We can portray the process that usually shapes our perspectives by employing a simple diagram:

Person ———→ World

Again and again, forgetting the limits of our perceiving, we look out at the world and believe that what we see is identical with what is there.[1]

Seeing and Believing

Actually our seeing is biased and selective because early in life our looking becomes biased and selective. A growing body of evidence argues convincingly that we perceive only what we have *learned* to perceive and that we perceive it in the ways we have learned to perceive it.[2] Psychologist George Leonard recounted a revealing conversation between a young boy, Bobby, and his mother. As I recall, the exchange begins when Bobby, who has just learned the names of primary colors, notices a blue aura about his mother's head.

"Blue!" Bobby observes, pointing to his mother's forehead, delighted to use his new knowledge.

"That's not blue!" his mother corrects. "That's my forehead."

Gazing intently at the aura, Bobby attempts again to share what he sees. "Blue!"

And, more firmly, his mother corrects him. "No, my forehead is *not* blue!"

Few children will try a third time, and if they do, they probably draw a strong reprimand.

Again Bobby points and says, "Blue!"

And his mother asks, now with exasperation, "What's the matter with you? Can't you see? That's not blue; that's my forehead!"

A child's perception is usually limited as the result of such encounters. Bobby learns that it is easier not to talk about auras—even though he sees them. Finally, Bobby stops seeing auras altogether. Leonard observed that children who stop talking about aspects of their reality eventually stop seeing those aspects as well.

The end result is a more complex mode of perceiving than what I illustrated in the simple diagram at the beginning of the chapter. Figure 1:1 shows a more accurate portrayal.

Figure 1:1 The "Framework" of Person A's Reality

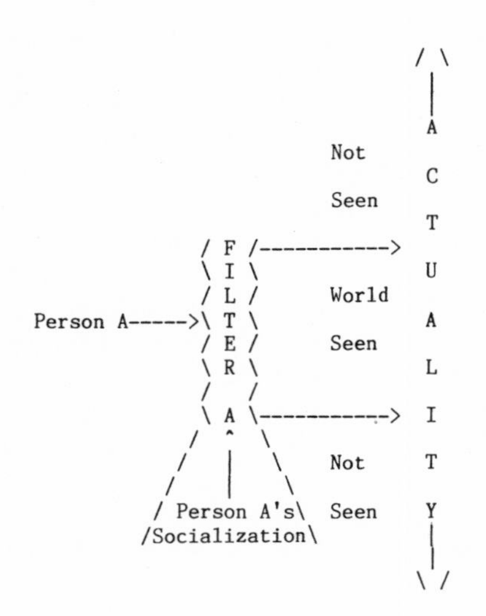

Continuing with Bobby as our illustration, we see that he learns first to deny and then to stop perceiving certain aspects of the actual world. As a result, the "framework" of perception he builds up, his "real" world, is a limited version of the actual world.

Bobby's "encounter" with his mother over auras is one example of a comprehensive process usually referred to as "socialization." Bobby's—and our—socialization can be defined simply as the sum total of all the influences that shape him—or us. These influences include not only what those around us intend to communicate to us, but also what they happen to communicate to us, both what we are taught and what we "pick up." Often the latter influences are at least as powerful as the former; hence the old adage, "What you are speaks so loudly that I cannot hear what you say." Or, as we sometimes observe, faith is not so much "taught" as "caught."

Consider analytically the process shaping Bobby's and our ways of perceiving the world. At least two factors are at work molding and limiting our perception. First, most of us deny some of what we perceive in order to satisfy our hunger for a predictable, orderly world. Second, most of us deny some of what we perceive in order to please (or make peace with) the authority figures ("significant others") in our lives.

We selectively simplify what is actually a complex world so that we can handle it more easily. Taking our cues from those who matter the most to us, we first organize reality and then fit new perceptions into our own general assumptions. Thus, we develop perceptual "benchmarks" (auras are not real; Mother knows what is real), which we use to order the world. The benchmarks function as norms, signaling what is real and what is unreal. *The* world is reduced to *our* world. We build a "framework."

This process, begun in childhood, continues into adulthood. In fact some of us discover that our early shaping is so tenacious that we cannot escape it, except with some difficulty, even when we very much want to.

I will use an illustration from personal experience. As far back as I can remember, I became somewhat anxious every time I traveled away from home. The uneasiness came over me just before I would leave on a trip and stayed with me until I returned. As much as I tried, I could neither talk myself out of feeling afraid nor identify why I was afraid.

I lived under the burden of those ill-defined fears for many years. Every trip included a tiring battle. Now as I look back at that time, I realize how I misconstrued the world. There was nothing in the actual world sufficiently threatening to justify the anxiety I experienced. Yet, even today, occasionally I vividly recall the discomfort I experienced during those years. How deeply I believed that there was something to be afraid of—even when I didn't want to and didn't know what it was.

In my young adulthood, as my work called for more and more travel, it became important to break free of these debilitating feelings. Several people were helpful to me—one especially, a Roman Catholic priest-therapist. For me, the combination he embodies made a difference. As counselor *and* priest he connected and unshackled me. The key words he offered were at first baffling and then startlingly clear: "You decided to believe that. You can decide to believe something else." And, with no little struggle and his superb encouragement, I did. For the first time I realized that *I* had made *my* world. I had decided what to believe and then become trapped by my beliefs.

Discovering that *I* decided gave me a new sense of power. It launched me into a period of new freedom and possibility in my life. Now I could permit the world to come through to me in new ways. I could examine what I had decided to believe (even when I had not been fully conscious of deciding) and choose to hold on to a belief or to believe in something different. As a friend said, "Well, you have finally grown up emotionally and theologically." (As this book develops I shall have much more to say about what has been stimulated by that observation.)

Of course, we do need to observe some caution: "growing up" isn't always that easy for me or, as I have discovered, for many other people. Using a descriptive slang phrase, we are all probably "hung up" at some points by our beliefs. These hang-ups are especially strong when what we believe is constantly reinforced by the culture within which we live.

Before considering the influence of culture, I will summarize what I have said to this point: Something intrudes between each of us and the world outside—a "filter" shaped by our accumulated psychological, social, and cultural experiences. Over time, as we perceive the world repeatedly through our own filters, each of us builds up a personal frame of reference that forms our perceptual "framework." This framework only imperfectly represents actuality because each of us is conscious only of what our own constructed filter will admit.

We simplify, organize, integrate our own reality. We don't remember what has happened to us so much as what our constructed frame of reference tells us happened. We fit the past into our own framework.

When confronted with meeting new people or experiencing new events, we consult our existing frame of reference to interpret the new. We fit the present into our own framework.

Likewise, our vision of the future: We believe that the new will fit into the old. We believe that what will happen will be consistent with our experience up to now. And even when it obviously isn't, we tend to force it to fit. We assume the future will fit into our own framework.

In this book I will be concerned more with the implications than the mechanics of this personal, world-building process—especially implications for our experiences of faith and church. Although many of us may want to resist the thought, we choose what to believe about God and church, just as we do about everything else: what we think God and church are like; how God and church fit (or do not fit) with all of life; whether believing in God or church is, on the whole, good or bad; whether God or church have any real influence in the world. We select, even though we may not be conscious of selecting. We choose, even when we believe our choosing is "inspired." Even when it is inspired.

Some of us have decided that God, as Christians traditionally have conceived of God, is real, makes sense in terms of our framework; others among us have decided that this God is not real, does not make sense. Some of us see the church as vital and significant; others see it as obsolete, irrelevant, misshapen, even harmful. Which is so is *not* similarly obvious to everyone and is less so as time goes by.

With the increasing pluralism of our society, what God and church are is no longer widely assumed to be readily apparent to anyone who cares to look, as most of us once believed, and as some of us still believe. Many of us have chosen to exercise the freedom my priest-friend helped me to discover. As a result, we think and believe differently. And, on the basis of our very different frameworks, we often discover that we believe in very different realities.

Becoming Acculturated

The psychological factors I have been describing function within a sociocultural framework. Each of us repeatedly reinforces her or his perspective with selective evidence received from other perceivers we have come to trust. Submitting ourselves to their continuing influence, most of us eventually notice *only the phenomena our group or culture has accepted as being real.* We become not only oriented and socialized, but also acculturated.

It may help us to understand how this acculturation process operates if we reflect on some cross-cultural experiences. I will begin by sharing one of my own.

As I relaxed at the piano one evening, playing through a collection of old show tunes, I came across a De Sylva, Brown, and Henderson song written for *George White's Scandals of 1931.* The lyric, set down more than fifty years ago, scandalized me in a way I'm certain the writers never intended. Yet night after night, I suppose, cultured audiences of white people heard it sung with no ill feelings about what they heard. It fit with the world as they had learned to see it.

"That's Why Darkies Were Born,"[3] the song's title, also serves as a refrain to convey its cultural message. According to the lyric, black people were born to pick cotton, to plant corn, and to sing and laugh, even when they were tired or abused.

Contrast this song's cultural perspective with another revealed in some patter from a routine by a black comedian—Dick Gregory, I believe. The dialogue, as I recall it, went something like:

> White people find it difficult to look at American history from the Indians' viewpoint. I tried to get some to look at it that way the other night. I came out of the theater and found a new, white Cadillac with the keys in it. So I drove away in it.
>
> The police stopped me down the road. They said, "You can't have this car; you stole it!"
>
> "No, I didn't!" I said.
>
> "Well, you have it."
>
> "That's true."
>
> "Then you stole it."
>
> "No, I didn't."
>
> "Then, how did you get it?"
>
> "I discovered it!"

Only recently have majority cultural perspectives been challenged enough for many of us to see how we abuse the minority members of our society (like whites taking land from the Indians while telling themselves they had "discovered" it). Many of us simply assumed that the world we saw is the world as it actually is, rather than the world as defined by our own cultural bias. Now we know that these culturally reinforced views are not only real, but may also be so deeply etched into our personal frameworks that they continue to influence us even after we decide to change.

A friend, in the early months after his elevation to a Roman Catholic bishop, was invited to preach the Reformation Day service at the Lutheran church in the neighborhood where he spent his childhood. In his opening remarks he described the feelings that had come over him as he walked toward the church that evening. When he was a boy, he told the assembled Lutheran congregation, his mother had warned him that Lutherans are "dangerous." To avoid the "danger" he always crossed the street each time he walked by this Lutheran church building. Although he had long since changed his view of Lutherans, as he approached the familiar church building this evening, he told them, the old feelings came on him with such force that he had difficulty keeping himself from crossing the street!

We are socialized within a culture. That culture impresses on us what we should accept and what is permissible for us to question. Thus, Bobby's mother tells him he should not see auras because the culture to which she belongs does not believe in auras. Through such intentional and unintentional messages he receives from her, he is socialized into that culture. More than likely Bobby discovers that most of those with whom he interacts share his mother's viewpoint. The collective reinforcement of what she says by many others stabilizes his socialization within *a* culture. Figure 1.2 shows the process.

Figure 1:2 The Cultural Framework of Reality

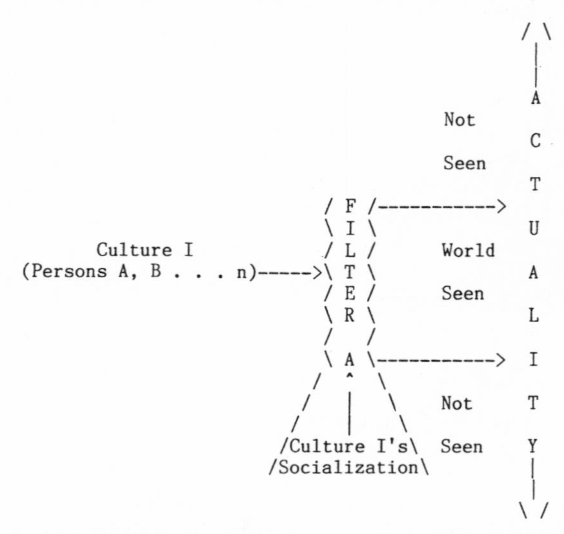

Bobby, his mother, and others share a common culture. They define the world in terms of that culture. Once they have defined "what things mean," their shared experiences serve to reinforce the cultural framework they share. They "know" what is real and what is not real. They even know why things happen as they do.

As we have seen, different cultures hold different assumptions about what is real and what is not real, as well as why things happen the way they do. Frameworks and the explanations they take for granted are culturally relative. Thus, those from one culture have difficulty accepting as real the explanations of another culture.

Bishop Lesslie Newbigin describes the difficulty of interpreting the reason for his involvement and serious injury in a bus accident soon after he arrived in India in 1936.

> [An] Indian pastor said, "It is the will of God." A Hindu would have said: "The karma of your former lives has caught up with you." . . . If I, as an "enlightened" European, had said that it was because the brakes were not working properly, that would have been—for the others—no explanation at all. It would have been simply a re-statement of what had to be explained. To speak of an "explanation" is to speak of an ultimate framework of axioms and assumptions by means of which one "makes sense of things." "Explanations" only operate within an accepted framework which does not itself require explanation.[4]

In a chapter titled "The Critique of Doubt," Michael Polanyi points out that cultures, like individuals, develop mechanisms to protect themselves against challenges to their frameworks.[5] He illustrates with experiences drawn from both modern and primitive cultures. He describes a circularity of logic that usually defeats the attempts of outsiders both to challenge and to understand the framework shared by members of a culture.

> [The] power of a system of implicit beliefs to defeat valid objections one by one is due to the circularity of such systems. . . . [The] convincing power possessed by the interpretation of any particular new topic in terms of such a conceptual framework is based on past applications of the same framework to a great number of other topics not now under consideration. . . . So long as each doubt is defeated in turn, its effect is to strengthen the fundamental convictions against which it is raised.[6]

Once a cultural framework is internalized and stabilized, it tends to survive even in the face of repeated challenges. Bishop Newbigin holds to his interpretive framework in India in spite of the fact that most other people in that country do not share it. He has "seen" other "accidents" that happened because the brakes on a vehicle failed. Likewise, the Hindu has "seen" other "misfortunes" that happened because the karma of someone's former lives caught up with him or her. Operating as each does within a different framework, the "explanation" to one does not seem to be an explanation at all to the other.

Similarly, Bobby's mother probably has heard of others who "imagined," mistakenly, that they saw auras. And she is concerned lest her son develop a "mistaken" view of the world. Their relationship works in favor of the cultural view she seeks to convey; his perception of her caring and concern encourages him to adopt her cultural view, even if doing so involves denying some of what he sees. In this manner his socialization encourages him to adopt the assumptions of the culture they share. Along the way he will probably encounter a few exceptional people within the circle of his interactions who do see auras. but they are exceptions. Of course, "exceptions," by definition, help to "prove the rule"—their "exceptionality" testifies to the accuracy of the overall framework.

To summarize: What we perceive, and ultimately decide, is plausible is not a result of our random, individual interaction with the world around us. What we conclude is plausible is the result of our internalization of certain fundamental, shared beliefs of our own particular culture. It is the result of our constant experience and repeated interaction with those who affirm that culture. When we share a culture we all believe in what we all see. It makes "common sense" to do so. When some of these fundamental assumptions in which we have always believed become questionable, we experience a crisis. Especially when we don't know what is wrong—or how to respond. And that describes what has happened to most of us over the past few decades.

The Challenges of Change

Once our framework is settled, we not only believe in it, but also depend on it. When something or someone threatens it we defend it. Under pressure, we rethink and revise, hoping to strengthen the way we approach the world within the framework we have come to trust. We want and need our framework to stand up.

In the early 1950s I decided I wanted to be a minister. I envisioned "minister" in terms of the cultural framework I had experienced. For me, ministry meant doing what I had always seen ministers do: praying, preaching, visiting, officiating. I saw the minister as a significant person at the center of community life. I kept this picture mostly intact during my years in seminary. On graduation I looked forward to a career of "ministry." My education had largely confirmed the traditional image of the church and the traditional role of clergy. Within a decade both were uncertain, if not broken. I was surprised, disillusioned, and sometimes angered by change.

I had, of course, seen some evidence of the change that was to challenge the viability of the traditional pattern I envisioned for myself when I opted for the ministry. So, I should have known better.

To begin with, while still a seminary student I was introduced to the "renewal" movement. A few of us were even regular participants in "small groups," wrestling seriously with how God could become more central to our and other people's lives. The colossal tragedy of World War II had raised some haunting questions: If God was "in control," how could God have permitted the evils of the war and the Holocaust? Why had the German church failed to raise the conscience of that nation to face the evils of the

Nazis? At the same time we were both enjoying and feeling uneasy with the popular religion and surge in church participation of the mid-1950s.

As we searched for answers we were challenged by some more radical ministers of the day, like Gordon Cosby of the Church of the Saviour in Washington, D.C.; a few of us even traveled to Washington to see firsthand what an authentically Chrisitan congregation is like.[7] We were deeply impressed by the commitment of those with whom we spoke—and by how few of them there were in a city the size of Washington. For my part, I wondered if a church and a minister had to be that radical to be authentically Christian. But I felt challenged because I did want to be a faithful Christian.

Only a few miles away from the seminary I attended, Dr. Norman Vincent Peale and the Marble Collegiate Church seemed to have adjusted well to the surge in church participation. He was preaching to hundreds at several worship services each Sunday and reaching millions more through his broadcast ministry and books. He reassured them all that God would help them "make it" in a changing time. (One man I knew then, who sold used cars to make his living, described how encouraged he was about his future since he had discovered God was going to help him sell cars.)

To aid those who were having great difficulty adjusting to the fast-paced society, the Marble Collegiate congregation developed an impressive counseling ministry. Based on the brief experience I had in the suburban church where I served as a student minister, I knew that many needed help. To keep pace with the growing need, some among my colleagues devoted themselves to "clinical training." I was tempted to join them, but uncertain; I wondered if a minister was supposed to be a therapist. But I did want to be a minister who could help people find strength and wholeness.

In the first months after my ordination some minister friends went off for a few days to a human relations laboratory. Some were quite enthusiastic on their return. They told of their newfound confidence; they had signed up for more training and encouraged me to do the same. They said we would be able to "manage" a large church well if we developed our "sensitivity" to people and our "OD" skills. As more and more churches became large, ministers would need the skills to design and manage complex organization and program. I soon learned what their jargon meant (OD stands for organizational development), but I was not comfortable with their picture of the minister as a kind of human relations expert-church manager. Yet I did want to help the church have effective program.

Then, at an area youth rally, I heard a sermon by Don De Young, a staff member of a New York inner-city parish. His attire—a clerical collar mounted to replace the regular collar on a gray work shirt—visibly supported his description of a sacrificial ministry in the urban "ghetto." He spoke of Christian "action." As I listened to him I wondered if I would have to be that intense and vulnerable to be a relevant minister. That question would face me more and more often as the social revolution, and the protest movement in general, grew during the years ahead.

Renewal, counseling, human relations/organizational development, social action: they all developed into full-scale attempts to strengthen the church in the face of change. Those committed to each approach identified a primary challenge and focused their efforts to address that challenge.

Challenge	*Response*	*Primary Concern*
Theological	"Renewal"	Faithfulness
Psychological	Counseling	Strength; health
Institutional	Organization; program	Effectiveness
Contextual	Social action	Relevance

Taken together, these attempts represented a massive effort to address the challenges of change. Yet, although each in turn burned brightly with hope for a time, they soon dimmed. Our combined responses were not sufficient. Most of us had a growing sense, year by year, that we were losing ground. And we were. Nothing we tried seemed to fix what was wrong.

The basic problems were beyond us. As time passed many of us recognized that we were not alone in our uneasiness and frustration. The society as a whole was struggling to keep the old framework intact. Even the politics of the time reflected the effort. In 1956 Dwight Eisenhower was again elected President, trouncing his opponent, Adlai Stevenson, for the second time. It was the general over the thinker. Eisenhower held woodenly to the old, cultural assumptions; Stevenson sought to describe how change was challenging our basic assumptions and requiring us to adapt. (I still have a volume containing his speeches and papers; one is called, quite descriptively, "Our Broken Mainspring."[8]) The general seemed to be saying that the old framework would hold together no matter what. Apparently most people wanted to believe him. (Although from the perspective of the present, his religious views seem incredibly simplistic, for example, "Every man ought to have a religion, and I don't care what it is.")

Overall, it was an abundant time for many. Yet, despite our relative economic well-being, there was widespread uneasiness, fueled by a sense of aimlessness. *Life* magazine and *The New York Times* collaborated on a series designed to clarify our "national purpose." It didn't—at least not convincingly.

In the church we had a similar uneasy sense of aimlessness in the midst of abundance. That was epitomized for some of us in the story of the precocious minister who returned to seminary five years after graduation to confront his ethics professor with the question: "Well, Dr. ———, I have built a church of two thousand members; now what do I do with it?"

In the 1960s and the years that followed the doubting got worse. These years are more vivid (and well documented) in most of our memories; thus, we can review them more briefly. Organized social change developed into a social "revolution." As that social change deepened and accelerated, critics pointing up the church's inability to respond adequately out of old institutional forms and assumptions became as rampant as they were articulate. Writers like Gibson Winter *(The Suburban Captivity of the Church)* and

Peter Berger *(The Noise of Our Solemn Assemblies)* initiated what would become a large literature pointing up the "irrelevance" of the church. Revolutionary dreamers, beginning with deeply committed church members like Martin Luther King Jr., enlisted the active participation of many dedicated Christians, especially the youth, in the causes of the social revolution. Soon both leaders and supporters were drawn as much from those beyond the church as from those within the church. Over the years the issues became less and less popular with most of those who continued to participate in local churches, as the protesters moved on from civil rights to such concerns as the war in Southeast Asia and equal rights for women and those who were homosexual.

Most of us who stayed with the church through these years (a good many clergy—some would say many of the "best" clergy—left[9]) experienced the gathering storm in the churches long before Jeffrey Hadden's book[10] helped to clarify the causes and nature of the disturbance. While some clergy were questioning traditional theology and breaking out of traditional ministerial roles, most lay leaders were defending the traditional framework: supporting orthodoxy, a traditional ministry, and the pre-social-revolution church. Making adjustments as they were able, most clergy tried to carry on with the definition of the church and ministry into which they had been socialized, hoping that someday things would return to normal. Few of these received much notice in the media; most of the notice went to the minority who were different, or who left the ministry.

The climax came for me, personally, in the mid-sixties. I became the senior minister of a large, suburban congregation. I moved from the rural congregation where I had been happy in my ministry to this church near the city because I believed that God wanted me to be closer to "the action." Fueled by my experience and reading in the literature of the renewal movement, I plunged into an effort to establish Bible study and prayer groups that would help people in the new church gather the wherewithal they needed to serve God in their work and community life. I had followed a similar approach in the small, village church where I served as pastor for seven years. There I worked closely with physicians, law enforcement officers, and others seeking to relate their Christian faith directly to their work. It seemed logical that those under greater pressures in an urban area would be even more eager to find support that would help them serve God in their daily lives.

I couldn't have been more misinformed. In the large church the small groups attracted hardly anyone. Moreover, my emphasis on relating God to "all" of life made them uneasy, especially when I became specific, commenting on current events engaging the community, like a labor-management impasse that led to a lengthy strike at the major manufacturing plant in that city. I wasn't "sticking to religion." The board told me to spend less time on the groups and more time visiting church members. Before long we were clearly at odds. I was suddenly in the middle of a conflict like I (and they) had been hearing about. The situation deteriorated rapidly. I could hardly wait to find a way out—which I did after a tenure of only twenty-six months.

At age twenty-four I had gone into the ministry with enthusiasm; a decade later I wanted to escape.

What had happened, and why? Looking back now, twenty years later, I see how thoroughly I misunderstood the nature and effects of social change on the church and its ministers, on those I served, and on me. I had not seen change in terms of the effects it was having on people's *basic* ability to function in all of life on the basis of the world as represented in their frameworks. I saw them only in terms of church. I did not see why most of them could not have done what I was asking them to do as responsible Christians, even if they had understood me. I (like most people in that time) was still seeing the world, as well as the church, in terms of the framework with which I had grown up. Misled by that framework, I overestimated the power of the church and the influence of the minister. I would not be able to change perspectives by stepping outside that framework until I lost some of my faith in it. And I would not be able to risk another perspective until I realized that neither God nor the church depends on the frameworks we defend.

Struggling with Inadequate Frameworks

Building a new framework that envisions the world and the church (and God) more accurately is precisely the challenge we face now. Wherever the old, relatively stable and integrated society continued, there was a consensus of support for the traditional framework that sees the local church at the center of life. Based on the model of a rural community or city neighborhood, it seemed realistic to believe that, up until the middle of this century, the church was in touch with most of life. For most people, most of what mattered was local. To them, it seemed logical to believe that the local church was informed about most of life, and therefore able to define overarching beliefs and values. Even those who were not participants in the church respected its position. Witness the honor and deference accorded to clergy throughout the first half of this century.

The rapid and radical social change of the past several decades has undermined both the social integration and the consensus of opinion that enabled the church, especially the local church, to function at the center of life. Few overarching moral and religious beliefs enjoy relative consensus today, especially when we attend to people's behavior. In fact, there is not even consensus within the church on many matters of belief and behavior. In an article titled "The Preacher and the Plumber's Son," John Baskin illustrates the impact of radical social change in a simple incident drawn from life in a small town—New Concord, Ohio.

> The change in the old order of things was announced on a Sunday morning on Thompson Avenue in the mid-fifties. It was not reported by the local press, and in the way that small

auguries attend large movements, it was little noticed by the neighborhood. On this particular Sunday, the librarian, Grace McClenahan, looked out her window and saw her new neighbor, the highway patrolman, come out to work on his house. She went over.

"This will not *do,*" she said. And by that, she meant the disreputable occurrence of work on the Sabbath. Neither work *nor* play were to occur on her Sundays. The New Concord grocer, as a boy, was not allowed to ride his tricycle, and the undertaker's mother recalled being whipped for sitting behind the stove reading the almanac. *Work?*

"Have a beer, Miz McClenahan," the patrolman said, "and let's discuss this."[11]

When there is a stable social order, people know their "place." They can find it. Sons and daughters can follow in their fathers' and mothers' footsteps because the trails are there to see. Everyone knows it is not right to work on the sabbath—even those who do it!

When social change takes hold, what is right becomes discussable. A lot of change leads to diversity. When diversity is evident, "common" sense is no longer common. People disagree about what is right.

The amount and variety of change over the past few decades is earth-shaking. The order of things today is qualitatively, as well as quantitatively, different from that of only fifty years ago. The world to which the local church related adequately is mostly gone. In the pages ahead we will need to admit to the new shape of the world in order to envision possibilities for faith and church. We will at least need to enlarge, if not replace, the framework with which most of us currently operate. To appreciate the need for such a radical step, consider a brief overview of the all-encompassing social change we have experienced during the past forty years.

In the middle of this century we lived through the "Age of Dislocation," during which one out of every three families moved their residence, most of them according to a similar pattern: away from rural areas into urban centers. The interrelated complexity of industrial technology requires a concentration of workers.

It also requires discipline and commitment. With the increasing focus of people's energy and commitment in the corporate sphere, the social influence of the workplace has grown to rival and, in the opinion of some observers, surpass the shaping power of home, school, and church.[12]

Geographic mobility has the effect of placing social distance between the generations, reducing the linkages of social accountability that have long provided the means for sharing culture (and faith) between children, parents, and grandparents.

Mobility places people next to each other who represent different (and sometimes conflicting) cultures and subcultures, like the highway patrolman and Grace McClenahan in New Concord, Ohio. As Bishop Newbigin discovered in India, living day by day next to those who think and believe differently can challenge one's own framework. And indeed has for most of us.

Some groups have challenged more than others. The "baby boom" generation, with its massive size, challenged the traditional social order. It developed its own identity, "in-language" (Are you with it), and culture—even its own "new math"—which parents were discouraged from attempting to master. Emerging communication technology, especially electronic media, encouraged a sense of solidarity and identity. Socialization came as much from within the generation as from guides in previous generations. Baby-boomers departed radically from traditional attitudes and behaviors in area after area of life, from school to work to leisure, to sex and religion. They continue to be distinct and unique, although recent economic reverses cast a disillusioning shadow in the lives of many of them.[13]

The medical technology that has emerged during the past few decades enables life to be prolonged, even when a body can no longer sustain itself and a person is no longer capable of awareness. It enables contraceptive methods to be so reliable that the unmarried can live together with only a remote fear of pregnancy. According to U.S. Census reports, the number of unmarried couples living together increased tenfold between 1970 and 1980.

The survey could continue for many pages. I shall look at those issues that affect the church and faith most critically in the chapters ahead. In summary, social change has been immense and comprehensive; it has radically altered our society and culture. And it has happened so rapidly that many, if not most, people have not been able to keep up. We suffer from that overall disorientation Alvin Toffler has ably defined as "Future Shock."[14]

Rapid social change has increased the distance between the local congregation and the diverse "worlds" in which its members now live. Wherever the old order still obtains (in rural areas, for example), church and minister are still present to all of life for most people. In the emerging, fast-paced, diverse, spread out mass society, especially in suburbs and other commuting residential areas, while men and most women go off to do the "business of the world," the minister and the church are left behind with the other women, young children, and older people.

Some church leaders, as we have seen, tried and continue to attempt to bridge the gaps. Only a few succeed, and most of these only temporarily. The idea that faith and church could have a direct role in all of life has become increasingly difficult for people to imagine. Now a generation has grown up, most of whom have never experienced the church as present to all of life. To see the church and God in such a way is not only difficult for them; for many it also seems absurd.

A few years ago, while I was a pastor seeking to clarify the significance of the church to all of life in the changing world, a socially astute church member offered to "tell it like it is," if I wanted to hear it. Carelessly I agreed. "The church is now a necessary luxury," he said; "you need it when your daughter gets married."

His comment made me angry. Actually, to be more accurate, it hurt, in the way painful truth hurts. We were struggling (he included) to hold on to the old reality our framework described, to make the church built on the assumptions of that framework function. We were having difficulty facing up to the collapse of that framework. We clutched at our few successes, like mine in the rural church, others in more radical congregations and ministries, and still others in growing churches based in even greater growing population centers. But self-deception simply postponed the day we would have to face reality. We really were losing ground. Steadily.

As the 1970s merged into the 1980s the "successes" became concentrated increasingly among groups who seem to me to be nostalgic or who evade, who appeal to those who seek to perpetuate the past in spite of change, or who seek to escape. (More about that when I consider strategies.) Today's church and minister are seldom in the center, even close to the worlds in which most people live. Nor could they be. The old framework that insists that they are or could be is out of touch with the world that now is.

Insofar as we continue to function on the basis of what our old framework tells us is so, in reality we function reflectively, as Figure 1:3 shows.

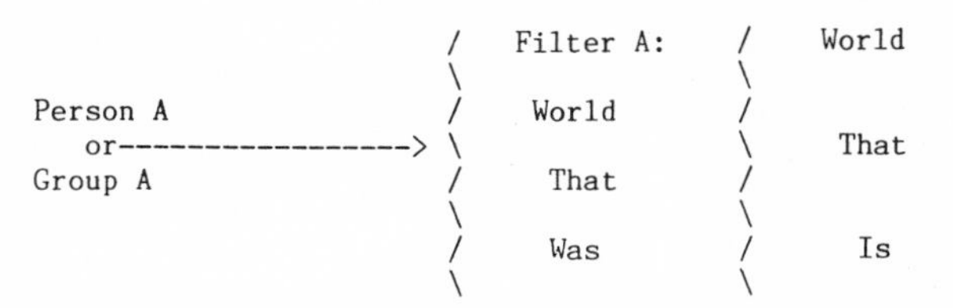

Figure 1:3 Reflective Framework

Our vision reflects and our framework is deeply influenced by a world we cannot forget—and still believe is fundamentally intact.

We think we see directly to the world that is; actually we see the world that is as it is reflected through our memory of a world that was. In the face of contradictory perspectives we may wonder which world is real. The multiplicity of frameworks in our time poses a confusing challenge both to believers and to the church, a challenge that will be explored in the chapters ahead.

In this chapter I have sought to describe how each of us constructs a framework, and to describe how some of us construct frameworks that are different from those constructed by others of us. I have suggested that a framework encompasses our picture of what the world and the church are and of what each can and should be. Finally, I have focused on the undermining effects of radical social change. How can we live and believe in a world where social change repeatedly calls into question what our framework tells us is and ought to be so? And suppose we have defined no alternatives. (Perhaps because we have always assumed we shouldn't or won't have to.) Suppose we don't know how to go about defining alternatives. What then? This dilemma is our circumstance today. And "What now?" our prime agenda.

CHAPTER TWO

Living in Spaces

As human beings, we have an immense capacity to adapt. We weather even aggravating changes that bring considerable stress to our lives. Slowly, often reluctantly, we incorporate new behaviors into our routine, often unaware of how different we are becoming. Then, unexpectedly, we are confronted by overwhelming evidence that the world around *us* is different from the world we normally envision. And we can no longer avoid seeing our own changing reality.

When the World Held Life Together

Some years ago the newspapers announced that the small grocery store in the center of the village where I then lived would be closed. Many residents responded with anger to the announcement, although most were also frank to admit that they purchased little from the store. That had not always been the case. Years before, when most people worked in or around the village, they bought their groceries at the village store. Now, with the exception of older residents, and a few others who did not have ready means of transportation out of the village, most residents stopped to buy their food (and most everything else) from supermarkets in one of the suburban shopping malls located along the routes they traveled to and from work. Purchases in the village grocery were reduced to those few items they forgot or used up unexpectedly in between their trips to the malls.

So, for all practical purposes, in most people's lives the local store's closing was of minor significance. Yet many were quite angry about the loss. Perhaps the loss represented more to them than the closing of a small grocery store.

Someone remembered a well-stained spitting stove that occupied a central place in the store "before the war." Out of service for many years, it nevertheless stood as secure reminder of a time when major decisions that affected everyone's lives were worked out by the local elders, who sat around the stove and chewed, leaving behind stains that testified to their dominant position in the community.

Until the central school was built three miles away, the village school had stood on what is now a park area across the street from the store. Each June the local weekly newspaper carried stories of class reunions held by those who attended the old school (along with "then and now" pictures of the graduates). Even now the school bus from the central school stopped in front of the village store to receive a dozen or so children, most of whom had arrived early to sit on the wooden steps and share the latest news. And later in the day, when the bus would bring them back, before they walked home, many would stop in the store to purchase some candy and catch up on what was now the latest news.

Of course, the store manager and his wife would experience the greatest disruption. They lived adjacent to the store, where at least part of the time both of them worked together. Their children left for school from the wooden steps out front and were among those who purchased some candy at the end of the day. When the fire whistle blew or some other emergency occurred, they were there to respond. When the local pastor needed to "check something out," the manager and his wife were always available—and faithfully in their pew on Sunday at the church down the block. This interwoven pattern of village life would come apart when the manager and his wife, in order to find work, were forced to join the ranks of commuters and, like most residents, become absent from the village most of each weekday.

Such an interconnected lifeway was not limited to rural areas. With the exception of certain downtown areas of "big" cities, this integrated way of life was as prevalent in city neighborhoods as it was in nonmetropolitan areas. I recall similar scenes from my own childhood on the west side of Chicago. When my father and mother married, they took an apartment in the neighborhood near the manufacturing plant where my father worked. Like most of those who lived in the houses nearby, he walked back and forth to work. Schools and churches were distributed throughout the neighborhood. Like their rural counterparts, those who lived close together were neighbors in most segments of their lives.

Probably the integrated pattern of life was disrupted sooner for many of those who lived in the city. The change for some was voluntary, as it was in my parents' instance; their financial situation improved, and they were able to purchase a home in a nearby suburb. As a consequence my father, too, became a commuter. In fact, when it came to church, we all did! Each Sunday we drove back into the city to attend the old neighborhood church, unwittingly helping to begin what most city churches would experience in years to come as a major problem: lack of a parking lot. Originally, none of them needed to provide much parking space; members lived close by and most walked to church, like they did to work and to shop at the local market. And for the convenience of those who lived a bit farther away, in those days the street cars ran on Sundays. Few of us are conscious of how much the space in which we live has changed until we can't find a parking place.

Within the integrated pattern of life in these classic American communities and neighborhoods, people were regularly and frequently in touch with one another—*and so were the primary institutions within which they lived their lives.*[1] Workplace and school building, police and fire stations, grocery store and church building were all within sight of one another—or nearly so. People felt the presence of all of them as they moved among them. That pattern of life is diagrammed in Figure 2:1.

Figure 2:1 Integrated World

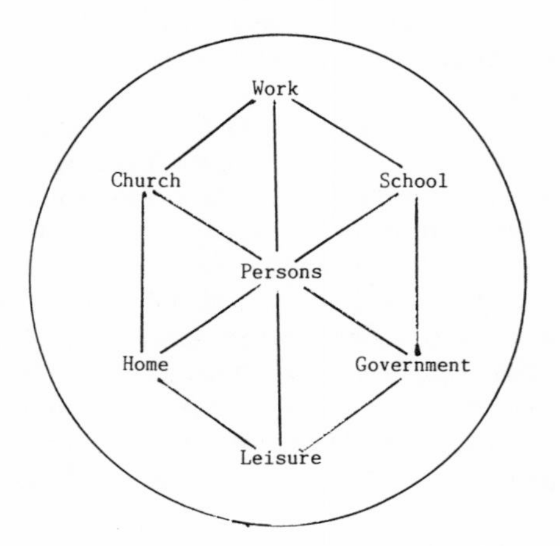

The same people moved through various segments of life together. Living within a restricted geographic area, most of them saw one another in several roles. Ordinarily, many of the same people worshiped, learned, worked, and played softball with one another.

The lines in the diagram are also intended to show the connections between institutions. (There should be lines interconnecting all of them, but that, although more accurate, would make the diagram too complex to follow.) At the beginning of each school day a child saluted the flag, listened to a scripture reading, and heard the teacher offer prayer—a direct daily reminder of the connection between school and nation and church.

Often the same people held power in several institutions and were able to foster the connections among them. I recall listening to a retired schoolteacher describe her experiences at the turn of the century in a small New York village. As a condition of employment she was required to live in the home of one of the trustees of the one-room school where she taught—obviously so he could see that all her lifeways were reputable. It was also understood that she would attend the local Presbyterian church, where the same man was an elder. He, along with the rest of the community, expected a schoolteacher to give regular evidence of her piety, as well as her knowledge.

By the late 1950s, when I became pastor of the church in a neighboring village, that little one-room school had yielded to centralization. Yet the connections between school and church were still very real, as I discovered soon after my arrival. Every other week throughout the school year one of the area ministers was expected to host a "character education" session held in the school auditorium. The term was a thin disguise for what was, in reality, religious instruction. We showed a religious film to the assembled students and teachers, and then, to be certain no one missed the film's message, the minister in charge reiterated it in a short sermon, followed by prayer. Not until the mid-1960s did someone challenge that arrangement, a challenge that the state department of education readily upheld, much to the consternation of nearly everybody in the community.

The entire interrelated network of village life was held together by a social force named "What-will-the-neighbors-think?" In such a community a person might doubt the pervasive influence of God; but the neighbors were clearly omnipresent. Everyone knew a neighbor could suddenly appear anywhere. It *might* be possible to evade their eyes, but transgressions were risky: one could never be absolutely certain no one would see.

Not that such an integrated world was entirely burdensome or oppressive. The pervasive social accountability also gave a sense of ease or freedom to relationships. Living with the same people in all parts of life, year after year, one knew what was expected and what to expect. Where the old system is still intact, so is the refreshing freedom, as I discovered a few years ago.

Despite all the modern equipment he uses to operate his large dairy farm, the farmer who cuts and bales the hay on the small farm my wife and I own represents the old "world." Several years ago I had a brief conversation with him during which we agreed on a price per bale.

Recently, a visitor from the city, with whom I shared the story of our "agreement," asked, "Do you count the bales?"

"No," I responded immediately and then realized that it had never occurred to me to do so.

"Then, how do you know you are getting what you deserve?" he went on.

"I know," I said, "because I know Wendell." When community life is integrated and affords the protection of reputation, we know where and with whom it is necessary to provide for our own personal protection by resorting to written agreements.

In a world composed of such relationships, people also experienced the local church as connected to all of life. Crowned often by a steeple that made it the tallest building around, the overshadowing presence of the church was evident to just about everyone. And at least one church building in each community or neighborhood was likely to include a clock in its tower. The hourly chime reminded people of the church's dominance. Even those who did not attend.

The pervasiveness of ministers reminded them as well. No communitywide event began or ended without a pastor's prayers. (In the early 1950s a minister friend, serving his first church in a small town, was startled to discover that he was expected to offer the invocation at the community Halloween parade.) Moreover, it was assumed that the minister had the right to visit anyone *unannounced*. This awareness, that the minister might appear at any moment of the day, was sufficient to keep most people on their toes, if not on their best behavior.

Except for the remnants we see around us, today this traditionally American way of life *actually* continues only here and there in those few neighborhoods and communities that change has passed by. Yet it is still real in the reflective frameworks to which many of us adhere. But as strong and as real as it may persist in our frameworks, it is largely a world that was. And therein lies a dilemma: except for a few of us, the world in which we believe no longer can be.[2]

Life Comes Apart

Several years ago I saw two pictures of the same area on Long Island, New York. The first was taken shortly before World War II; it showed acre on acre of potato fields, with hardly a house in sight. The second was taken about 1955; it showed *all* those acres covered with row on row of nearly identical houses, with not a single row of potato plants in sight.

The story of urbanization in our country, the fact that we have become predominantly a nation of cities and suburbs during this century, is well known to most of us. So much so that I do not feel the need to detail the demographic and economic and organizational changes once again. Most of us require little convincing of the reality of urbanization; the structures and roads and massing of people now compose our daily experience.

But the ways our personal perspectives have been reshaped as a result of our experiences in this new world are not as clear. What has happened to our frameworks as a result of all this massive change? How do we see and experience life differently? How have we adapted, and at what cost?

In the mid-1950s, as a young minister in the rapidly growing suburbs of New York City, I often had a sense that those with whom I worked in the churches were not comfortable with the changes into which they had been thrust by the times. Many had rural or small-town roots. When they were recollecting these roots, often they talked longingly of "some day" being able to go "home" again. As I worked among them it became increasingly apparent to me that they wanted their pastor and church to function like the rural pastors and churches they remembered—and missed. Year by year I found those expectations more inappropriate and difficult to sustain in the radically different suburban-urban world. Besides, with my big-city roots and no rural experience and my lack of appreciation then of the role nostalgia can play in people's lives, their insistence on what I saw as a dysfunctional pattern seemed more and more pointless.

Nevertheless, I continued to discover how much they wanted to hang on to the old world. As I became involved in an area committee concerned with new church development, I encountered yet more (and very visible) evidence. When it came time to build a church building amid the seas of split-level houses, most building committees chose the same style of church—colonial; the majority of church buildings constructed in this era resemble the village churches of an earlier time, except they are larger. People seemed to want a new colonial church to match the new colonial furniture with which they were furnishing their homes. They craved reminders of their roots.

So, week after week, congregations without a single farmer among them sang hymns filled with rural, pastoral images as they worshiped in large, new church buildings designed to look small and old. None of it made much sense to me then. In retrospect I have better understanding; I see a generation struggling to hold on to its bearings in the face of overwhelming change.

And more empathy. Now that I have had a sustained rural experience and more opportunity to appreciate the overwhelming effects of social change in people's lives, I am not inclined to be as critical of this generation's struggle to stave off the effects of change wherever it could. The contrasts it faced—and with which we all now live—are drastic.

Life has come apart. The store manager's experience has been replicated in the lives of millions. A disconnected, disintegrated life has become our routine. Daily life, which formerly took place within an integrated community or neighborhood, is now, for most people, composed of separate segments, each isolated from the rest. For most of us, the particular activities of work, school, home, leisure, and church are carried on in different places. We reside in one place, go to school in another place, go to work in another place, go to ski (play) in another place, go to shop in another place, and go to church in another place.

Only each individual is in touch with the diverse experiences of all the segments of his or her life. Once the store manager goes to work in a large factory, his life at work is no longer accessible to family members, except, perhaps, on special occasions when visitors are permitted into the plant. No one, including his pastor, can simply drop in. What we do at work is hidden from those at home and at church. When I moved from serving as a local pastor to become a synod executive, I joined the ranks of the commuters. Some years later one of my sons told me he thought I had left the ministry at the time of the change (he was ten then). "I didn't know anymore what you did."

Only each individual can appreciate what it is like to live in (through?) *all* these separate places. No one else knows. No one else shares all his or her experiences firsthand. The task of keeping it all together, balancing the demands of each segment with the rest, constructing a manageable life, falls almost entirely on the individual. Hence the commonly used slang exchange: "How are you doing?" "Oh, I'm keeping it together." Individualism is no longer a choice for most people; it is a functional necessity.

Keeping it together can be quite difficult. First, there is the well-known burden of commuting from home to work, and to school, and to shop, and to play, and to worship, and to do whatever else one does. A good bit of our energy is consumed in transit.

In addition, those in each segment tend to conceive of individuals to whom they relate there only in terms of the experience they have of the individual *in that segment*. The only dimension of a person's life they see firsthand is what they see in that segment. When they function out of such a limited perspective, those in authority in a segment may unwittingly add stress to a person's living, especially if they are not sensitive. Quite early we have to become adept at juggling conflicting pressures.

Consider the situation of Tom, a thirteen-year-old. Those at school see Tom as "student." To be a "good" student, he should do his homework and attend band practice regularly, as well as all football games when the band performs. Teachers at school seldom have direct experience of the additional obligations that press on Tom in the other segments in which he lives.

Those in charge in other areas of Tom's life are likely to be similarly shortsighted. At church the minister sees Tom as a "confirmand" and believes that for Tom to be a "good" church member, he should attend the scheduled weekly confirmation class—and, of course, worship on Sunday.

The coach and teammates in the soccer league see Tom as "team member"; they remind him that no other activity should interfere with the big game that has now been rescheduled to Sunday morning because of the rain on Saturday.

The members of his family see Tom as "son" and feel that he should be with them on Sunday when they go to see Grandmother, who is not feeling well and lives in the neighboring town.

While perceptive others may offer some support, Tom alone feels the overall burden and responsibility to juggle satisfactorily the conflicting demands of his life: how to play in the soccer game, attend worship, prepare for Monday's math test, and visit Grandmother, who is ill. Separated in isolated segments, these conflicting obligations interact only in his person. There are few, often no, other lines of communication among them.

By using a diagram (Figure 2:2), one can illustrate the segmented world in which Tom and most of the rest of us now live.

The "person" at the center of the diagram is singular. Each individual now stands alone at the center of his or her life. Each person still moves from segment to segment as he or she did in the integrated community or neighborhood. But now each moves as an individual. He or she seldom relates to the same people in the various segments of life. Different activities take place with different people at isolated locations, each some distance from the others. There is no longer a truly "local" community, a place where people carry on all or most of the activities of their lives together.

We know from various studies of urbanization that much of the stress with which we contend is a result of the increased size, scale, and pace that characterize nearly every dimension of life today.[3] Everything is bigger and harder to keep up with than it used to be.

But we also have less personal and local control in many of the segments of our lives. A friend who served on the school board in the same district where the old teacher began her career near the turn of the century shared his frustration at the board's lack of control over the affairs of the now-centralized school district. "Just about every decision we make is mandated by the state," he complained.

William Goodwin describes this phenomenon of increasing size *and* decreasing local control in organizations as "scale-up" and points out its pervasiveness throughout the segments of our living.[4] He also describes some of the dangers that can accompany the centralized control that goes with scale-up. *Scale-up compounds the problems that stem from the segmentation of life, especially in segments that are highly organized.* With scale-up, those who have authority in the organizations and institutions that compose each segment tend to value the organization as a whole more than the overall welfare of the persons in a particular locale.

Not long ago the area where I live suffered the effects of such a callous decision. The dowel mill located about a mile from our church was purchased by a large timber corporation. After only a short time, the management decided that the local mill was no longer "profitable" and on a fall Friday gave all workers notes with their paychecks stating that the mill was closing as of that day and that they were no longer employed. Workers had no advance notice, no opportunity to negotiate options (like finding a buyer, or purchasing the mill themselves and continuing to operate it).

With increased organizational size and scale-up, distance increases between individuals and those to whom they are ultimately accountable. Often those with final authority in an organization have no direct contact with those who are affected by their actions and decisions. It then becomes much easier to view people solely in terms of their contribution and usefulness to the organization.

"Let the buyer beware!" takes on an especially ominous note when

Figure 2:2 Segmented World

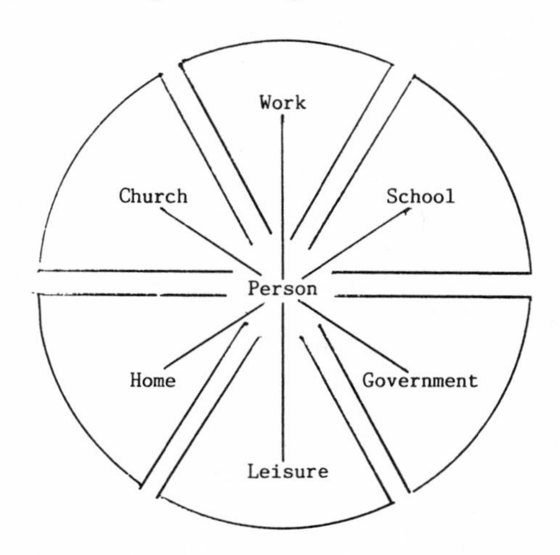

buyer and seller are no longer in direct contact. Commenting on a case of alleged misrepresentation in advertising by one of the nation's largest retailing chains, the attorney general for the state of Maine noted that his office has special responsibility to protect consumers when they lack direct access to the company that institutes practices that may be abusive to them.[5] Employees in the local store who deal with customers have little control over company policy. They may be as powerless as the customer.

Not even the church is immune to the problems associated with scale-up. When I served as a national church executive, I often heard local church leaders complain about the insensitive and unrealistic manner in which the national church dealt with local churches and their leaders. Now that I am out of that office and a regular participant in a rural, small congregation, I am chagrined to discover how often I agree with my former critics!

In its most powerful form, the process that combines scale-up with disintegration can become as insidious as it is abusive. Writing several years ago in a *Fortune* magazine article entitled "The Wife Problem," William H. Whyte shares some revealing remarks made by senior management officials of one of the largest U.S. corporations. The company founder describes their policy toward wives: "Our wives are all part of the business. We started with just a few hundred people in 1914 and decided that no matter how large we grew we would carry it on in the family spirit. We always refer to our people as [our] 'Family' and we mean the wives and children as well as the men."

The company provides "family" members with a country club, complete with golf course, bowling, tennis, facilities for picnics and parties. All for $1 a year. But as another company official makes clear, the real price tag is much higher: "Successes here are guys who eat and sleep the company. If a man's first interest is his wife and family, more power to him—but we don't want him."[6]

Today it is unlikely that one would make such a blatant (and sexist) statement of company policy toward employees and their families. Admittedly, there has been some improvement in the attitude many organizations take toward their employees as persons.

Yet such remarks may also be uncommon today simply because it is less necessary to offer them; many employees have accepted the powerful influence of the corporation or organization throughout their lives as a given. Such dominance may not be as apparent to us now as when it was first being established because we have come to expect large organizations to exert this kind of control in our lives. We have adapted our living and adjusted our frameworks.

Whenever authority is scaled up, in government, work, school, or church, the organization transforms a segment into a realm, sometimes blatantly, sometimes subtly. When faced with such bureaucratic power, we are, in reality, "subjects." When our values are challenged or violated by the demands of the organization, we feel, and often are, powerless to change the way we can live in that segment as long as the organization dominates.

Sometimes the dilemma comes into focus when the conflicting values of two segments come together. A minister friend preached on the text "You shall not kill." After the service, as he stood at the door shaking the hand of a church member, he was surprised to hear him say that he was going to quit his job "as a result of what you said in your sermon."

Startled that someone would contemplate such a drastic step as a result of his sermon, my friend asked if he could stop by that afternoon to talk over the decision with his parishioner. When they conversed later the church member reminded his pastor that he was a research physicist who helped design nuclear power plants. Such power plants are used in submarines. Submarines carry missiles. "Missiles kill people!" he blurted out. "It all came together for me in church today."

"I even tried to talk him out of his decision," my pastor friend went on, "but I couldn't. He said he hoped the church would understand and support him." He could no longer comply, and he saw no way he could continue to live in that segment under the dominion of that organization without complying.

Much of the time we take advantage of the space that isolates the segments of our lives to avoid such conflicts. When we "go to" work, school or church, travel to each usually involves traversing considerable distance. We use the travel time to prepare ourselves for the transition to the different life we will have to live in the segment to which we are traveling.

One friend, who for fifteen years commuted an hour each way from home to work, changed jobs and moved to a new location where the office was only a ten-minute drive from his home. He confessed it took him months to adjust. "I simply was not ready to be home in ten minutes." The family learned they had to give him time to prepare to reenter.

Such scheduling has become important to most of us. We juggle the multiplicity of demands by carefully scheduling our movements from space to space. We describe our scheduled times as "commitments," a powerful word originally used to specify the *overall* boundaries of a person's life. Commitments to various segments are routinely associated with specific times. In each of these times we are committed only to the activities of a specific segment.

For example, when we are "at work," we normally are protected by being at the "workspace." Similarly, when we "go backpacking" or "go home," we are protected from normal obligations associated with other segments, like work. Specific activities, relationships, obligations, and protections are associated with specific times and places. We specify boundaries against intruders. "Don't call me at work!" "She's not available, she's gone on vacation." "He isn't here; he has gone to church." When living in one segment we feel protected from obligations associated with another. (The implications of that feeling for our understanding of church are, of course, important, as can be seen in the chapters ahead.)

Given this segmented, spacially defined pattern of life, it seems quite understandable that many of us internalize the assumption that certain behaviors are appropriate, even that certain behaviors *are possible only* in certain segments. Thus, we learn at school, work at work, play at the ski area, and worship at church. It is only one more step to believe that we can learn only at school, work only at the office, play only when we go skiing, and worship only when we go to church. And then, that it is not possible to learn well except at school, to work well except at the office, to play well except at the ski area, and to worship well except at church. And finally, that we are obligated to learn only at school, to work only at work, to play only when we ski, and to worship only at church.

We now have a new world that requires a new framework. This world is composed of distinct segments around us. The segmented living that was characteristic of only a few persons (e.g., the rich and well born) in past eras is now pervasive. Most of us are now faced with the need to envision the world within a new framework. We know, at least to some degree, that our lives are segmented *and* lack connections.

But the transition to a new framework is not simple—even for those of us who experience the segments of life as fragmented from the beginning—at least from the time we begin our daily rides on a school bus. From the first we have been surrounded by those who believe in the endurance of the old order, especially if we have been closely associated with the church. In spite of our experiences of the actual world around us, we may not *want* to believe the old order is fatally broken. Traditional elements persist in many, if not most, of our frameworks. As a result, many of us find it difficult to define satisfying ways either of living or of believing.

Adapting to a Segmented World

In chapter 1 I noted that a key characteristic we share as human beings is our hunger for order, and that to satisfy this hunger we simplify the world by developing categories of perception. To maintain our internal order, we may even force the actual world into our categories, overlooking what does not fit with what we believe is so. Also, we tend to trust and associate mostly with persons who share our particular world view.

When we live in an integrated community or neighborhood, we generally find external support and confirmation for an integrated framework. The shape and the manner in which that world ordinarily functions reaffirm the cohesive framework within which we perceive it. The segments of our lives are experienced as interconnected because they are open to one another. We tend to interact and move with the same persons as we progress from segment to segment. Our life is integrated without and within.

When we contrast that world with our present fragmented life, it is not surprising that many of us find living in the contemporary world stressful. We contend regularly with powerful and conflicting demands in a variety of segments or realms. Resolving these conflicts is often not within our power. Complying is not only expected, but sometimes required, especially in realms like work and government, where powerful authorities are present.

How do we adapt to life in such a conflicted and disintegrated world? And what happens to us as human beings in the process of that adapting? In what remains of this chapter I will describe several approaches we may take and what I see happening to those who pursue each. Then in chapter 4 I will examine how the church attempts to help us deal with the difficulties that emerge from living in a segmented world.

1. Some of us perceive (or pretend) that nothing, or at least very little, has changed. As much as possible, we keep on living as we always have. This option functions best for those of us whose framework was shaped when or where the old order of community was intact (or believed to be intact). This option is also more workable for those of us who, because of location and life-style, are not as vulnerable to social change.

For example, on the one hand, someone who represents the third generation to operate a family-owned insurance agency, who interacts frequently with other business people, the community's attorneys, the school principal, and the local ministers, both at chance meetings on the street and regularly at the weekly meeting of the Rotary Club, is more likely to perceive the old, interconnected order of community life as still in place. His or her daily life reflects the old order. Such a person is more likely to see the contributions of church and community organizations as significant and possible.[7]

On the other hand, someone who leaves the community to travel for an hour to his or her office, who several times each month attends meetings in distant cities, who in the course of the workday seldom encounters anyone from the community where he or she lives is more likely to perceive the world as a collection of unconnected realms. There is little opportunity to experience the interconnections in chance meetings with those who represent other segments, at the Rotary Club, at the children's concerts at school, and at meetings of church organizations. The reality of unconnected realms is reinforced continually in this person's experience. Such a person has fewer opportunities to see how church and community organizations touch life as a whole. In fact, he or she experiences them as distant from much of life. He or she finds it much more difficult to pretend that the old integrated order is still in place.

On the whole, the more restricted a person's living is culturally or geographically, the easier it is for that person to perceive or pretend that the integration of life continues.

2. Others among us deal with the stress of living in unconnected worlds by withdrawing as much as possible from those realms where we experience the most stress.

A few years ago, when I was serving as pastor of a large suburban congregation, I received an unusual letter from the former pastor of a man whom I shall call "Peter" (not his real name). Peter had recently moved his membership to my congregation. His former pastor apologized in the letter that several months had elapsed since he sent me the official transfer for Peter. He then went on at some length, listing Peter's vital contributions as a lay leader in his former church.

I was surprised. In the new congregation Peter was distinguished by his inactivity. He attended worship but had steadfastly refused every invitation to become more involved. Armed with the letter I confronted Peter at home. Why had he not been equally active in his new church.

His response was not the excuses I expected. He said simply: "I have been moved four times because of my job in the last ten years. In each community up until this one I have become deeply involved with people and organizations. Then suddenly, in each place, I have had to tear myself free of important commitments and deep relationships. It has all been so painful that I have decided not to become involved locally anymore. It's just too costly to leave."

People like Peter reduce the stress of living in unconnected segments by becoming only marginally involved in some. One invests heavily in work and family, only a little in church. Another invests heavily in church and work, but only a little in family. A third invests in community life and family, but only a little in work and church. Such a way of life takes no little emotional juggling to sustain—and the cooperation, or at least the tolerance, of those in the marginalized segments.

Of course, insensitive persons in authority can contribute to the stress that people experience. As noted in the previous section, authorities in each segment may see persons narrowly, solely in terms of their contribution to that area. One church member, active for years in the organizational life of his congregation, shared this dilemma. He had recently been elected to the town council. To find time to attend council meetings and related committees, he reduced his activity in church organizations. After the worship service the previous Sunday, his pastor had drawn him aside to express concern about his recent "neglect" of his church work. He was angry at the pastor for his narrow vision and suggested that he widen his view of "church work."

Not everyone is able to respond with such strength. We all know those who suffer stress-related diseases, from ulcers and colitis to hypertension, because they believe they should be able to fulfill all the expectations of those at work, at home, at church, in the community. So, they overwork and sometimes compromise their values. And feel alone in their plight. Often they are because no one sees them all together.

3. A third approach to living in a segmented world is taken by those who seek to segment themselves interiorly into many "selves."[8] We distinguish ourselves differently in different segments.

One example of this approach is the "open marriage" movement, more popular a decade ago than it is today, although it is still widely practiced among some groups in the U.S. population.[9] Participants tend to be drawn primarily from among those who are liberal in moral outlook, who live fast-paced lives within a variety of segments, who regularly travel considerable distances among those segments, and who spend considerable time away from home. Lacking the time (or desire) to build a primary intimate relationship with one person, they built intimate relationships with several persons. Each of these relationships does not necessarily include a sexual dimension, but sexual relationships are not ruled out.

Advocates of this approach describe the variety of intimacy in their lives as enriching. The lack of social accountability that marks our society today and the tendency for many people to remain single even into their early thirties combine to make simultaneous and unconnected intimate relationships possible for a goodly number of persons.

Critics of this approach include not only those who question it morally, but also those who have found multiple intimacies impossible to sustain, or who have found the quality of their marriage relationship compromised by other intimate relationships. A variety of intimate relationships takes considerable orchestration, as well as tacit understanding among the various persons involved.

4. Moving in a direction quite opposite to those who seek to find intimacy in several segments, others among us seek to resolve the dilemmas associated with living in unconnected segments by consciously restricting our relationships and the space in which we live. Currently such efforts are apparent in the migration of people out of metropolitan regions into rural areas, and in a few remaining communes.

Communal living arrangements among young adults attracted a good deal of attention during the 1960s, when they were novel and most popular, especially when their members held radical political views and exhibited unconventional sexual behavior. With the passing of time we have seen many of these communes disappear. In fact, except for those communities that include a clear, religious commitment, most communes do not survive more than a few years.

But in spite of their limited ability to persist, communes appear to be an attempt to counter the effects of distintegrated living. Members choose to confine themselves to interactions with a few persons with whom they carry on the various functions of life and with whom they spend most of their time. Like the monastic orders and religious sects with which we have long been familiar, the common commitment of the members of a commune provides them with a way of life that offers many of the benefits we associate with a traditional integrated community.

The "small groups" that were especially widespread in the two decades from the middle fifties to the middle seventies seem to be a less radical form of commune. Encouraged by a variety of agencies, including the church, these groups appear in several forms. Some are specifically religious ("prayer" groups or, in a more complex form, "house churches"); others embrace a more general range of topics ("discussion" groups). A common thread seems to run through all the groups: the concern to bring some coherence to life—coherence of action, but if that is not possible, at least a coherence of shared understanding.

A similar, but much more general movement is the "New Ruralism" that began in the 1970s and persists into the present time. Calvin L. Beale, a demographer with the U.S. Department of Agriculture, was the first to call attention to a reversal of the rural-to-urban migration that has so marked the movement of our population during this century. "Under conditions of general affluence, low total population growth, easy transportation and communication, modernization of rural life, and urban populations so large that the advantages of urban life are diminished, a downward shift to smaller communities may seem both feasible and desirable."[10]

There is a point at which the disintegrating effects of urban living become so costly that some, perhaps many, people are willing to exchange some economic affluence in order to gain what another student of the trend terms "psychic affluence."[11] During the late 1970s, while conducting a study of leaders in small rural churches, I interviewed some of these "refugees from the urban sprawl," as one of them characterized the movement. This articulate young man in his middle thirties described his pilgrimage from a major metropolitan area to a small community in upstate Vermont. His story followed a typical pattern. He told of his frustration and then disillusionment as he attempted to deal with the issues of living in an urban area. Finally, unable to "get it together there," he moved to the small community where he presently lives. In animated terms he described how much better his life has become since the move. "Life is manageable here. . . . I can get at things that matter. . . . I have some control over what I do."

Looking back on that interview I see now that much of his hunger was for integration. Although he had given up a significant amount of income, he told me repeatedly that he had gained even more in the sense of wholeness and integration that marked his life in this rural area. He, and many others who have migrated to nonmetropolitan areas believe that such a recovery of community more than compensates for their reduced economic affluence.

Not everyone is able (or willing) to find a satisfactory source of income in a rural area, but the latest U.S. Census (1980) indicates that a growing number of persons are willing to commute over great distances to work in order to cluster the rest of their living in a more restricted area. Such persons seek to interconnect the segments of their lives to a greater degree than is possible in metropolitan living.

5. A fifth approach to resolving the dilemmas associated with unconnected living is probably the most common, as well as the most popular, among church members. When we follow this approach we choose one segment as primary and devote ourselves as much as possible to that area of life. The language that people use to describe us, and with which we identify, often testifies to the segment that is primary for us: "She's a homebody." "He's a church worker." "She's a workaholic."

The way we spend our available time also testifies to our primary devotion, especially what we are willing to let spill over from one segment into the others. Devout workers "take work home" (a very descriptive phrase). Devout church members meet in a prayer group during their lunch hour at the office. Devout parents take time away from their work to be with their children. Devout volunteers spend time in church and community organizations to the neglect of their families and work.

Devotion to a segment can become so consuming that a person redefines herself or himself *as a person* in terms of roles expected or advantageous to fill in that segment. Often as a pastor I have been aware that those

WHOLE INTEGRATION CENTERS
PARTS FRAGMENTATION BOXES

who spend a great deal of time "at church" see them*selves* fundamentally as church workers. So do those around them. A wife will say of her husband, "I can't get Charlie to do anything around the house; he's always fixing something at the church."

Even though they were helpful at the church, sometimes, I as a pastor, was uncomfortable with the devotion of such parishioners. As I came to know them better, I realized that many of them were spending so much time at the church to avoid spending time at home or at work.

Once we identify ourselves with a segment, what we do in that segment may consume us to the point where we lose perspective on our life as a whole. So people say, quite accurately, "He's lost in his work." "She's a church nut." "He lives to ski."

Because the unconnected segments tend to be autonomous and out of touch with one another, they lack the connecting checks and balances that integrate life in a traditional community or neighborhood. Some segments may even exert abusive power over vulnerable individuals who invest themselves.

Although people may submit themselves almost totally to any segment, work is probably the one most often chosen. Several factors encourage that choice. To earn our living, most of us must spend a great deal of time at work. We also draw a great amount of personal significance and identity from our work. When asked, "What do you do?" many of us will respond by describing our work, for example, "I am an accountant." And, as noted earlier, authorities in the work realm can exercise a great deal of power. We need to earn money to live. Many of us also believe that we need to succeed to be significant. When others have the power to decide how much we will be paid and whether we will progress, we may go to great lengths to become what we believe they think we should be.

In a classic article entitled "The Meaning of Work in a Bureaucratic Society," Joseph Bensman and Bernard Rosenberg describe the process. Although their language is, unfortunately, sexist, they paint a vivid picture of the personal hazards of primary devotion to work.

> In an employee society, "personality" becomes a market commodity, one that has measurable cash value in terms of present and future income to its possessor. Once the alert bureaucrat recognizes this, he sets out to acquire his magic key to success. . . .
>
> Self-rationalization appears when the official begins to view himself as a merchandisable product which he must market and package like any other merchandisable product. First, an inventory is necessary. He must ask: what are my assets and liabilities in the personality market? What defects must be banished before I can sell myself? Do I have the right background? If not, how can I acquire it? With such questions, the inventory is converted into a market-research project. The answers give him findings with which to remodel his personality. The bu-

reaucratic personality is molded out of available raw materials, shaped to meet fluctuating demands of the market.

Old habits are discarded and new habits are nurtured. The would-be success learns when to simulate enthusiasm, compassion, interest, concern, modesty, confidence, and mastery; when to smile, with whom to laugh, and how intimate or friendly he can be with other people. He selects his home and its residential area with care; he buys his clothes and chooses styles with an eye to their probable reception in his office. He reads or pretends to have read the right books, the right magazines, and the right newspapers. All this will be reflected in "the right line of conversation" which he adopts as his own, thereafter sustaining it with proper inflections. His tone is by turns disdainful, respectful, reverential, and choleric, but always well attuned to others. He joins the right party and espouses the political ideology of his fellows. If he starts early and has vision, he marries the right girl, or if he has been guilty of an indiscretion, he may disembarrass himself of the wrong girl. Every one of these procedures is a marketing operation—with its own imponderable hazards. If the operation succeeds, our official will have fabricated a personality totally in harmony with his environment; in a great many ways it will resemble the personality of his co-workers. . . .

[This] . . . process, however, requires denying other portions of the self. Officials strive to develop those aspects of their personality which fit the bureaucratic milieu. This makes it difficult for them to develop aspects that are "out-of-phase." Hypertrophy in one direction spells atrophy in another. One consequence of self-rationalization as a technique to control personality is that, after some time has passed, the poseur may find that he is a different person. With much practice, "control" becomes unnecessary; the bureaucratic mask becomes the normal face, and refractory impulses get buried beyond reactivation.[12]

Perhaps such overall devotion to work, and the resulting reshaping of an entire life to succeed, is uncommon today. Some may disagree with Bensman and Rosenberg's portrait, pointing to a growing appreciation of the employee as a whole person on the part of more enlightened supervisors in many corporations and other work organizations. Perhaps.

It is equally possible that we have now become more accustomed to conforming. During the dozen years from 1967 to 1979, when I served as a church executive, I knew I was expected to subordinate my community service, my activities as a local church member, and my family life in order to be free to travel extensively, and to give fifty-five to sixty hours each week to serve "the church." At the time I envisioned my sacrifices in the rest of life as made in order to "serve God." Now I realize that I redefined myself as a person primarily in terms of what was expected of me in the work realm. My god was not God, but the church. Most clergy who "serve churches" are quite familiar with the feelings and the process.

The process can become insidious, especially when total devotion in a segment is touted as a high standard everyone should honor. I recall listening to a group of devoted church members advocate such a commitment. They began by outlining the vital ministries in which they engage. Their church is primary, they told me repeatedly. When obligations of their work come into conflict with their church obligations, they will risk loss of their jobs to fulfill their church commitments. For example, none of them will accept a new job that involves leaving the area where their church is located. When a husband or wife of one of them is not involved in the church, the spouse has to come to terms with the primacy of the church member's commitment to the church. All conflicts between church and the other segments of life are resolved in favor of the church. They quoted scripture (largely inappropriately, in my view) to support their primary commitment to the church. When I suggested that they had turned their church into a god, they became quite defensive. Obviously I had struck a blow at the core of their identity. In the pages that follow I shall question both the efficacy and the theological soundness of such a resolution that favors even the church segment above all others.

To summarize: In our segmented world, identity is no longer a given, but a product. Rapid and radical social change has disrupted the old, interconnected social pattern on which we formerly could rely for support and protection. Each of us alone sees the dimensions and interactions of all the segments in which he or she lives. Although others may help us, in the last analysis we must discover for ourselves how to "get it together" and "keep it together."

The next chapter shows that, unfortunately, such attempts to integrate our living and believing are compounded by the fact that we are now as unconnected in time as we are in space. Social change has disrupted the old, familiar, generation-to-generation developmental pattern most of us assume dominates human socialization. Now we are just as much unique, products of our own times as we are of the homes and families and communities into which we are born.

CHAPTER THREE

Living Through Our Own Times

When I was a child I didn't like asparagus. I recall one occasion especially when I was touting its lack of better qualities to my grandmother, boasting that *I* would *never* eat it. She replied with the age-old adage: "Wait until you put your feet under your own table!" In other words: "When you are paying for the asparagus, you will eat the asparagus." Her prophetic words impressed me little then; I reiterated with great emphasis, "*I* will never eat asparagus."

Now, fifty years later, I have gained respect for her wisdom—and not only because I relish asparagus. I have discovered, as do most people, that I experience life (and asparagus tastes) differently in middle age than I did in childhood.

Shaped by Our Own Times

We not only age; most of us also develop. In the process of developing we reconsider some of our initial perspectives. Sometimes we sample again what we once experienced as distasteful and discover that because we have changed, we now experience life differently.

Such an analysis of human growth assumes that we not only age, but also *develop,* and accumulate some wisdom as we do so. It assumes that we are wiser when we are twenty years of age than when we are ten and, likewise, more at forty than either at twenty or at ten. As each year passes, we have the benefit of more accumulated experience. Speaking out of such a frame of reference, parents have advised children for generations, "Someday, when you grow up, you will see that the world is as we say it is."

Traditional cultures especially include the belief that those who are older are also wiser. Young people are taught to give respect and authority to those who are the "elders." The elders have lived more years and accumulated more wisdom and are, therefore, better equipped to offer sound guidance.

What may not be apparent within these assumptions about older and therefore wiser is the primary assumption that the world (and the church) in which we live does not change, or changes slowly. Only with no or slow change do older and wiser necessarily go together. But suppose the world changes rapidly and substantially—as it has in recent decades. What happens to the elders' ability to offer sound guidance to the younger generation?

Then we find ourselves in circumstances where the developmental model and the authority of the elders to instruct those who are younger are both challenged. As Margaret Mead suggests in her book *Culture and Commitment,* until recently the elders could legitimately defend their superior insights with the suggestion "You know, I have been young and *you* never have been old." (But now such is often not the case.) "Today's young people can reply: 'You never have been young in the world I am young in, and you never can be.' "[1]

When the world changes radically, human beings encounter radically different experiences as they pass through the same developmental stages of life. They move chronologically through childhood, youth, and so forth on into old age like the generations that preceded them. But their experiences of the world are qualitatively very different at similar life stages.

What is more, in important ways they never let go of the experienced differences. They form and reinforce a different framework; and they continue to perceive and define the world in terms of that unique framework as they progress through their lives. Thus, they not only experience the developmental stages of their lives differently, because they form and maintain unique perspectives, even when they are mature *they perceive the same experiences differently from those socialized previously, who are now side by side with them in the same period*. In important respects they never grow up to take on the same perspectives their elders hold. They become a "cohort."

A cohort is composed of contemporaries who share experiences that uniquely and fundamentally shape them. People outside the cohort not only do not share these experiences; they also lack certain basic frames of reference needed to interpret them in the way the cohort interprets them.

For example, one of my sons attended the notorious Woodstock rock concert of the sixties. When he returned I asked him, "What was it like?" He replied, "If I told you, you wouldn't believe me."

His reponse was neither unkind nor patronizing, but simply a fact. He was clear that I lack certain frames of reference necessary to accept his description as accurate. His experience of youth was not only different in time from mine, but also different in culture. I do not share the framework of his culture. I am a member not only of another generation, but of another cohort as well.

I belong to my time and my son belongs to his time. Each of us has had fundamental experiences we can talk about but cannot share. To rephrase slightly his response to my question about the rock concert: "If I told you,

you couldn't believe me." In the face of dramatic social change, what members of one cohort believe easily, members of another find impossible to believe.

In the same way that members of different ethnic groups are ethnocentric, members of well-defined cohorts are "chronocentric." Those within a cohort experience and interpret the world through their own times. For example, those in their late fifties and early sixties (agewise) and those in their late thirties and early forties each experienced a war firsthand: World War II and the war in Vietnam, respectively. For those directly involved, the gore and horror were similar. But the overall frameworks within which each war is interpreted by each cohort are, at key points, very different. As different as the World War II song "Praise the Lord and Pass the Ammunition" and the Vietnam era "protest" song "Ain't Gonna Let Nobody Turn Me Around."

Those who fought World War II did so with a sense of support from the entire society. Their sacrifice was constantly held up by those of us back home as courageous and honorable. They were our heros, defending our civilization against evil powers.

Those who fought in Vietnam struggled against the backdrop of a divided country at home. The country was by no means united behind them, especially their contemporaries, many of whom saw their battlefield struggles as futile, if not immoral. They returned from the horror of war to a homeland more often seeking to forget what they had done than to welcome them as heros. Many still struggle to affirm their own integrity.

The difference between the two cohorts is as much a matter of interpretation as it is of experience. Accepted interpretations within each affirm or malign the same values. What is commonly accepted within each cohort reinforces the cultural framework of that cohort. Of course, not all whose age places them within a cohort share the general attitudes of the cohort; some intentionally choose not to be included. But a majority identify themselves with their cohort's attitudes and assumptions. And nearly all those within a cohort understand one another in ways that outsiders do not—even cohort members who dislike the commonly held attitudes.

Becoming a Cohort

How do contemporaries form such bonds of understanding and begin to experience themselves as a cohort? When do they develop a chronocentric framework?

To begin with, a cohort is not the same as a "generation," although people commonly use the word generation to describe a cohort, as, for example, when speaking about the "baby boom generation" or the "Depression generation." Well-defined cohorts may or may not occur within the interval required biologically to produce a new generation. A new cohort can emerge within such a twenty-five year interval, or it may take forty years; or, with rapid social change, a new cohort can emerge in as little as a decade.

A potential cohort becomes an actual cohort "only where a concrete

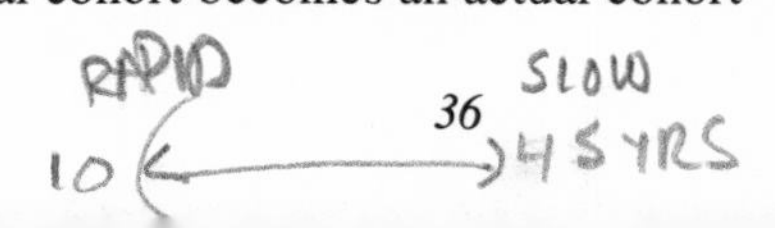

bond is created between members of a generation by their being exposed to the social and intellectual symptoms of a process of dynamic de-stabilization."[2] At a critical stage in their development (I shall describe that stage presently) certain dramatic events uniquely and fundamentally shape the interpretive framework of generation members. They experience these events as social "traumas," and thereafter interpret life through a framework shaped during these "de-stabilizing" experiences.

In recognition of these traumatic shaping events we often name cohorts for their crises. We speak of the "Depression" or "war" generation, or of the "sixties" generation. We know that each of these cohorts went through key experiences at critical times in their development, experiences that continue to affect them.

In much the same manner that we assume other elements that compose our frameworks, those of us within a cohort usually take the cohort's interpretation of the significance of key experiences for granted. Unless someone outside the cohort questions us, we are seldom conscious of our chronocentric assumptions.

Several years ago I was presenting material describing how the experiences of the World War II cohort shape the way in which members approach believing and the church. I repeatedly referred to "the war." When I was well into the presentation a young man in his late twenties stopped me with the question "Which 'war' are you talking about?" He was one of only a few in the group who were under age forty-five. For the majority of us there was only one war—World War II. We were surprised by the younger man's question.

Then, during the discussion period, he made our experience of distance from him even worse. As we reminisced about "those terrible times" we all remember "just like they happened yesterday," he commented in an unbelievably (from our viewpoint) detached manner: "It all sounds just like history to me; you could just as well be talking about the Spanish-American War."

"Oh, but you don't understand!" we pleaded.

"You are right," he admitted. And we knew he couldn't. Not really, because he wasn't old enough to have been there.

At a certain point in our development, usually during late childhood or early adolescence, certainly by age eighteen, most of us psychologically "leave home." During the next few years we increasingly break free of the constraints of childhood and the confinements of family. More and more we turn to our peers and certain significant others beyond the family for information about the larger social and cultural world that surrounds us. For several years, until we are in our early twenties and well established in young adulthood, our frameworks are molded by fresh impressions we gain from the culture that surrounds us.

In his pioneering essay on cohort development, Karl Mannheim suggests that this stage in our acculturation continues until the point at which language and dialect are fixed. Mannheim points to research indicating that when adolescents move into a different environment, they

> readily assimilate new unconscious mental attitudes and habits, and change their language and dialect. The adult, transferred into a new environment, consciously transforms certain aspects of his modes of thought and behavior, but never acclimatizes himself in so radical and thoroughgoing a fashion. His fundamental attitudes, his vital inventory, and, among external manifestations, his language and dialect, remain for the most part on an earlier level.[3]

When these fundamental years of acculturation to the larger world include social crises, our fundamental picture of the world is usually shaped dramatically by these crises. To use Mannheim's word, these crises "de-stabilize" us. And for the rest of our lives we distinguish ourselves by the sympathetic bonds we share with others of our own time, who were similarly "de-stabilized." With them we know together how and why *we* are different. In countless, subtle ways we (to use the common, slang expression) "read" them and they us. As again and again each of us describes fundamental shaping events to others, we discover that only our peers in time seem able to appreciate how these key events reveal the basic nature of the world. Together with the contemporaries who compose our cohort we forge a chronocentric framework. With them we see the world, past *and* present, through that shared framework. We share a culture in time.

To recall the church group I described earlier in this chapter, those of us who at the time (1980) were over forty-five years of age had to come to terms with the fact that the young man and his peers can't share our framework because he didn't share our fundamental shaping experiences. We and he are of different cohorts. We and he experience the world through different fundamental perspectives, forged during different "prime times."

Once we mold a chronocentric framework, year after year we strengthen our unique perspective by interpreting additional experiences in terms of that framework. We move along through life seeing and experiencing selectively. Taking our cues mostly from the (as we see it) more reliable perspective of members of our own cohort, we reinforce what our "prime-time" framework encourages us to see and experience. Wherever our framework has been shaped by social traumas we affirm it most vigorously to challengers outside our cohort, at times even denying the reality of the others' perspective. We persist in our own time, even when the world around us no longer confirms what we believe. We function through a "reflective" framework. (Recall Figure 1:3 in chapter 1.) We see what is through our unique, lingering experiences of what was.

Twentieth-century Cohorts

There are three distinct cohorts living side by side in the present time. I call them Strivers, Challengers, and Calculators, and date them historically according to the listing in Table 3:1.

Table 3:1 Twentieth-century Cohorts (by Age)

Cohort	*Born*	*Age 13–22 in*	*Core Years*
Strivers	1901 to 1931	1914–1923 to 1944–1953	1919 to 1949
Challengers	1932 to 1954	1945–1954 to 1967–1976	1950 to 1972
Calculators	1955 to	1968–1977 to —the present—	1973 to

Strivers were born from 1901 to 1931. Their basic acculturations in time (years when they were thirteen to twenty-two years of age) ranged over the years from 1914 through 1953, a thirty-nine year period dominated by war and depression.

Challengers were born from 1932 through 1954. Their basic acculturations in time ranged over the years from 1945 through 1976, a thirty-one year period that began with victory, dreams of general affluence, and optimism but that concluded with economic and social retreat, and, for many, general disillusionment.

Calculators were born from 1955 through the present. Their basic acculturations in time began to occur in 1968, when the most precocious of those born first reached age thirteen, and continue into the present. From the outset most of them have experienced the world more soberly than the generation that preceded them, as a place where only those who are able to make wise choices thrive. Perhaps even only those who are privileged, or fortunate.

In Table 3:1 I have purposely overlapped the borders between the cohorts. Transitions from era to era and from one cohort to another do not occur in an instant. Some adolescents make the shift at an earlier age than others; they are more precocious and move out beyond the dominant influences of home and into the larger world at an earlier age. Those who live in some geographic locations experience the effects of social change earlier than those who live in others. For example, as already noted in chapter 2, people in urban areas often experience change before those in rural areas, and those on the east and west coasts of the United States, before those in the center of the country. Finally, some individuals are more radical, and quicker to adopt change, while others lag, taking on the new patterns much later. A few persons never adapt, stubbornly holding to the attitudes of a previous time despite the differing views of the majority of their contemporaries.

To provide for these varying rates of change, I have indicated several years of transition between cohorts. Once the midpoint of these years of transition has passed, most people take on the attitudes of the new cohort. The years from midpoint to midpoint are shown as the cohort's core years.

The last column in the table shows the core acculturation years for each cohort: the twenties, thirties, and forties for the Strivers; the fifties and sixties for the Challengers; and the seventies into the eighties for the Calculators.

For more than a decade, following the theory advanced by Mannheim, I have interviewed members of each cohort and asked them to identify key events that occurred during the years of their primary acculturation. Such events are their self-identified, "unforgettable experiences," or, to use Mannheim's word, "de-stabilizing" events that jolt cohort members during the years of their initial acculturation. The perspectives defined during these events continue to shape the way cohort members see the world.

Most people quickly identify to which cohort they belong when certain key words or phrases evoke strong feelings within them. For example:

Strivers are gripped by:	The Dust Bowl
	The Depression
	Dunkirk
	Pearl Harbor
Challengers by:	"I have a dream!"
	Woodstock
	Kent State
	ERA (Equal Rights Amendment)
Calculators by:	Three Mile Island
	Hostages

Those outside a cohort may also find their feelings aroused by key words that are connected with prime-time experiences of that cohort, but they are generally not emotionally jolted to the extent that cohort members are.

Members of a cohort reidentify themselves when they hear their own key words and phrases. They are clear again about who they are and what is basically so. Once again they reinforce their reflective framework.

In Figures 3:1, 3:2, and 3:3 I have listed key events that members of the three cohorts alive today describe consistently as fundamental in shaping their common framework. First the cohort I call Strivers (Figure 3:1).

The arrow to the right of Strivers indicates that they look at the world through a reflective framework shaped by the events listed inside their filter. The primary shaping events that Strivers recall center about war and the Depression. Often they refer to themselves (and others to them) as either the Depression generation or the war generation. The years that formed and followed their primary acculturation were dominated by massive efforts to survive against nearly overwhelming odds.

Those outside the cohort often have difficulty appreciating the incredible challenges the Strivers faced. Consider:

During the years 1929 through 1931 stock losses alone topped $50 billion; 1,000 banks failed. By 1932 more than 12 million persons were out of work.

More than 2,300 persons were killed in the Japanese attack on Pearl Harbor. German bombs killed 70,000 British civilians. Some 18 million members of the armed services were killed in World War II; in all, 45 million persons lost their lives.

Nearly every Striver alive today was touched directly or is (was) related to someone who was touched directly by World War II. Strivers vividly recall a massive effort, total commitment together, a complete mobilization of all the nation's resources to win that war. Hard work and working together are core values and core elements in Strivers' functioning. In their experience we survived as a nation and as individuals only because of our superior commitment and way of life ("American way of life").

Most Strivers believe that people who commit themselves together to a worthwhile goal or a just cause usually achieve their ends—and deserve to—even in the face of overwhelming odds. Russell Baker's autobiography of his childhood during the Depression, *Growing Up,* provides a revealing picture of how Strivers learned to survive. Not only is he repeatedly goaded to achieve by his mother's repeated injunctions to make something of himself in a world that offers few opportunities and meager resources; he is also inspired by her powerful example as a widow, struggling to earn the means to provide for them and maintain the family's honor and respectability in the process. Once cannot help but be moved to admiration by Baker's description of the two of them on a winter's day, pulling a coaster wagon laden with

Figure 3:1 Striver Framework

Prime-time and Shaping Events

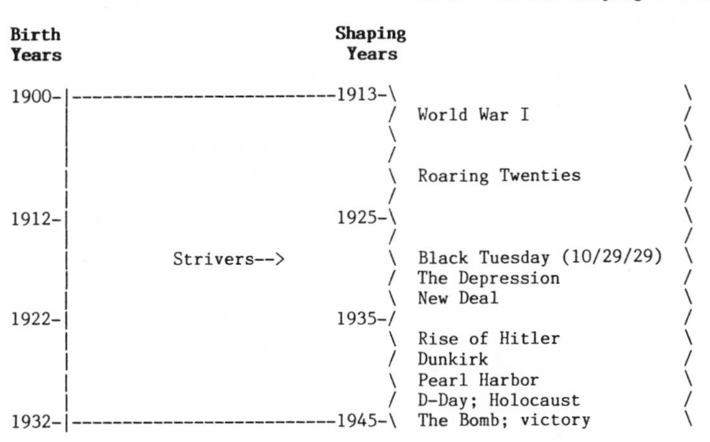

some goods received from welfare, taking off their coats to hide the goods from the eyes of their neighbors, in order not to compromise their respectability.[4]

Similarly impressive is the 1944 motion picture *The Fighting Sullivans.* It chronicles the late Depression/World War II experiences of an Irish Catholic family. All five sons enlist in the U.S. Navy after the attack on Pearl Harbor—but only after the Navy agrees that they can serve together on the same ship. The father mortgages the family's house to pay all the sons' debts before they leave. ("There's never been a mortgage on this house before.") A year later, when the naval officer who had enlisted them arrives with the tragic news that all five have been lost when their ship explodes and sinks (because four brothers refuse to abandon the fifth who is wounded and in the sick bay as the ship explodes), the father controls his grief and goes off to his work as a freight conductor ("I have never missed a day's work in thirty years"), while the mother controls her grief to make coffee for the officer who has conveyed the sad news. These are classic Strivers: strong, proud, self-disciplined, sticking together and to their appointed tasks in the face of any adversity life brings.

For those Strivers who do survive the difficult years, there is finally victory, and even affluence. The years after World War II are better, an economic boom time. But Strivers still hold to their basic, prime-time functioning even after the need for striving is passed. They continue to work hard, ready to protect themselves from some future war or depression. Their reflective framework feels more solid than "novel" occurrences in the present.

Strivers' inability to give up striving is not shared by the cohort that follows them. The Challengers' prime-time acculturation begins in the midst of the victories that Strivers struggled to win. Figure 3:2 shows the contrast between their beginnings and those of Strivers.

Challengers' prime-time acculturation starts with a taste of victory and a hefty meal of affluence. Their childhood comes in a privileged time. They see mostly the victories of World War II, without the long years of struggle and sacrifice. Economic growth in the 1950s and 1960s soon follows, bringing an unprecedented abundance of consumer goods. Many Challengers are born into homes that both want them and are able to provide them with the best, materially.

And there are a lot of them. From 1945 through 1964 the U.S. birthrate soared; during most of these years the number of births approached or exceeded 4 million. By the mid-1950s the sheer number of persons in the Challenger cohort had in itself become a destabilizing experience.

Such large numbers in their cohort encouraged Challengers to develop an unusual sense of their own power early in their lives. By the mid-fifties they were determining the fads: $100 million of Davy Crockett hats and rifles and T-shirts and records in 1955; 20 million Hula-Hoops in 1958. The Boomers became Challengers. Suddenly *they* defined what was in and what was out. In the 1960s, as hordes of Boomers became teenagers and their taste for "rock" displaced Tin Pan Alley tunes in the Top Ten, even the

Figure 3:2 Striver and Challenger Frameworks

```
                                          Prime-time and Shaping Events
Birth                       Shaping
Years                        Years

1900-|------------------------1913-\                                 \
     |                             /  World War I                    /
     |                             \                                 \
     |                             /                                 /
     |                             \  Roaring Twenties               \
     |                             /                                 /
1912-|                        1925-\                                 \
     |                             /                                 /
     |          Strivers-->        \  Black Tuesday (10/29/29)       \
     |                             /  The Depression                 /
     |                             \  New Deal                       \
1922-|                        1935-/                                 /
     |                             \  Rise of Hitler                 \
     |                             /  Dunkirk                        /
     |                             \  Pearl Harbor                   \
     |                             /  D-Day; Holocaust               /
1932-|------------------------1945-\  The Bomb; victory              \
     |                             /  Baby boom                      /
     |                             \                                 \
     |                             /  Suburbia                       /
     |                             \                                 \
1942-|                        1955-/  Affluence                      /
     |          Challengers-->     \  Hula-Hoops                     \
     |                             /  Civil rights movement          /
     |                             \  New Frontier                   \
     |                             /  J.F.K. assassinated            /
1952-|                        1965-\  Urban crisis ("Watts")         \
     |                             /  Vietnam                        /
     |                             \  R.F.K., M.L.K. killed          \
     |-----------------------------/  Woodstock; Kent State          /
```

venerable Hit Parade was pushed aside. The Hit Paraders are simply not up to the music of the Beatles and the Rolling Stones.[5] Soon most institutions and corporations of American society, from family and school and church to record, toy, and clothing makers, clamored to meet the Challengers' needs and cater to their desires. No wonder Challengers expected to change the world!

They tried. The narrow victory of John Kennedy in the election of 1960 and his vision of a New Frontier, coupled with the dreams of civil rights leaders like Martin Luther King, fed their dream of remaking society. Their sexual freedom and use of drugs frightened, and sometimes scandalized, their Striver parents. But Challengers were heady with endless potential, confident they could do everything.

Then came the shot in Dallas, and another in San Francisco, a third in Memphis, and a volley at Kent State. From 1963 to 1967 several prime articulators of the Challengers' dream—John Kennedy, Robert Kennedy, and Martin Luther King—were assassinated. And in 1970, at Kent State University, soldiers in the service of the U.S. government killed and wounded college students who were protesting what they saw as immoral acts of that government. By the end of the decade the heady vision of the early sixties had given way to disillusionment, even cynicism, that would transform many, if not most, Challengers into Retreaters during the seventies.

Challengers probably overestimated both their own human potential and the economic capacity of the country (and the world) to support their vision of an abundant life for all.[6] Whatever the causes, the reverses continue to be real. Many Challengers now struggle both economically and personally.[7] Perhaps their own numbers helped to produce the reverses that Challengers have come to experience. The same numbers that gave them the power to set trends in a time of increasing abundance have thrown them into competition with one another in a subsequent time of limited resources and continued economic stagnation. In their prime time they have experienced the combined destabilization of unparalleled affluence, followed by economic and social retreat. As a result, Challengers struggle with a reflective framework that gives them mixed messages about the world.

Not so the Calculators—at least not yet (1986). Their prime-time acculturation begins during the retreat years of the Challengers and continues through years of limited resources, as the events listed opposite them in Figure 3:3 show. Even early Calculators, who were born during the later baby-boom years (1955 through 1964), do not entertain the optimistic visions of the early Boomers.[8] Quite the contrary, even in early childhood they find themselves in biting competition with their peers.

Limits appear quickly and turn up everywhere in the Calculators' experience. In their growing-up years millions of Calculators become children of divorce, living with one parent, commuting between families as their parents remarry. Most enter already overcrowded schools. In their teens they are confronted with more experiences of limits, like frustrating hours waiting in long lines to buy gasoline. The nation's efforts to rescue hostages taken by Iranian extremists are bungled, and the hostages' release then stalled for months. The Equal Rights Amendment fails to be enacted in spite of repeated polls indicating a majority is in favor of it. The previous cohorts' vision of cheap and safe nuclear power enters the Calculators' experience in the long delays and cost overruns of Seabrook, the near-catastrophe at Three Mile Island, and the tragedy at Chernobyl.

Most Calculators now believe that few of them will have or achieve everything they want. Core experiences in their prime-time acculturation shape them to believe that they must choose among different options, hard choices that lead to very different outcomes. As a result, many, as the name I have given them suggests, calculate carefully, focusing their efforts in careful planning designed to achieve and protect what they want.

Even the Yuppies (*y*oung, *u*pwardly mobile *u*rban *p*rofessionals), who are among the highest-achieving Calculators, recognize that they, too, must carefully choose and plan to gain whatever they want most: *either* an outstanding career *or* an outstanding marriage; *either* a two-career household *or* children. And they see similar, mutually exclusive choices for our nation as a whole in a time of increasing threats and shrinking resources (e.g., we cannot have both an adequate defense system *and* an adequate

Figure 3:3 Striver, Challenger, and Calculator Frameworks

```
                                                   Prime-time and Shaping Events

Birth                              Shaping
Years                               Years

1900-|-------------------------1913-\                                  \
     |                              /  World War I                     /
     |                              \                                  \
     |                              /                                  /
     |                              \  Roaring Twenties                \
     |                              /                                  /
1912-|                         1925-\                                  \
     |                              /                                  /
     |          Strivers-->         \  Black Tuesday (10/29/29)        \ World
     |                              /  The Depression                  /
     |                              \  New Deal                        \
1922-|                         1935-/                                  /
     |                              \  Rise of Hitler                  \
     |                              /  Dunkirk                         /
     |                              \  Pearl Harbor                    \
     |                              /  D-Day; Holocaust                /
1932-|-------------------------1945-\  The Bomb; victory               \
     |                              /  Baby boom                       /
     |                              \                                  \
     |                              /  Suburbia                        /
     |                              \                                  \
1942-|                         1955-/  Affluence                       /
     |          Challengers-->      \  Hula-Hoops                      \  That
     |                              /  Civil rights movement           /
     |                              \  New Frontier                    \
     |                              /  J.F.K. assassinated             /
1952-|                         1965-\  Urban crisis ("Watts")          \
     |                              /  Vietnam                         /
     |                              \  R.F.K., M.L.K. killed           \
     |------------------------------/  Woodstock; Kent State           /
     |                              \  Gas lines                       \
1962-|                         1975-/  ERA                             /
     |                              \  Widespread divorce              \
     |                              /  Three Mile Island               /
     |          Calculators-->      \  Terrorism; hostages             \   Is
     |                              /  ERA ratification stalled        /
1972-|                         1985-\  "Star Wars" defense system      \
     |                              /  Shuttle explodes; Chernobyl     /
     |                              \                                  \
```

network of social services for all). Many are attracted to national leaders who emphasize protection (national defense, a stable economy, less emphasis on civil rights) rather than to those who are committed to the justice concerns so dear to the previous cohort. Calculators expect to live out their lives amid limits and are concerned to protect themselves and their ability to choose what limits will prevail over their lives.[9]

The three cohorts that live side by side in our time see the world uniquely in terms of their own frameworks. Through their varied, chronocentric perspectives they see different possibilities and experience different constraints. And, as the chapters that follow show, there are unique elements in their approaches to believing as well as to living.

The Shaping of Our Frameworks

The basic framework out of which most people function as adults is a result of the combined shaping force of their initial, childhood experiences and their later, cohort-related experiences. When a society is relatively stable the shaping received in childhood provides the adult with reliable suggestions for functioning in the adult world. In such a society most people discover the truth of Mark Twain's observation that when he was sixteen years of age his father seemed to him to be a fool; but when he had turned twenty-one he was startled to discover how much the old man had learned in five years.

Cohort-related experiences are especially influential in times of rapid change. When the world changes radically we are more likely to receive dependable cues about how to live from those within our own cohort. In such a society, radical social change undermines the traditional process of elders passing wisdom along to younger generations. Cohorts emerge, and members of each reflect experiences unique to their own prime time.

Thus, our adult frameworks are products both of our socialization as children and our socialization with peers who compose our cohort. This process for twentieth-century cohorts is shown in Figure 3:4. The diagram plots, first, childhood years, during which members of each cohort develop basic elements in their frameworks. Then it shows their adolescent years, when, as they enter the larger society, they are most vulnerable to destabilizing experiences that grow out of radical social change. The resulting adult framework reflects the choices individuals make about what is real while resolving the conflicts between their original childhood socialization and the destabilizing experiences of their cohort's prime time.

Thus, Strivers are initially oriented by those who act out a turn-of-the-century life-style, largely dominated by endless hard work. Early Strivers especially recall parents who struggled day after day simply to survive. They remember vividly how their parents labored to survive on marginal farms, in urban sweatshops, and in other, equally demanding settings. The "Careless Twenties" are a brief, untypical interlude, soon paid for in the destabilizing adversity of depression and war.

The long, drawn-out years of stress are so deeply etched in many Strivers' experience that even when they achieve (as many do during the postwar years), they can't quit striving. In fact, in my conversations with them, many Strivers now recall the years of adversity and scarcity, when they had to work hard and pull together simply to survive, as *good* times, as the "best years." Even when they achieve affluence and no longer need to strive, many Strivers say, "I don't know what to *do* with myself." Their choice of words shows they are still dominated by early experiences.

Strivers' childhood and prime-time experiences appear to be confirmed by their experiences in adulthood. Although they are deeply affected by depression and war, their experiences during prime-time years do not contradict the experiences of their childhood. "Our side" wins the war; and in the years that follow many Strivers realize the fruit of their hard work, as they achieve their educational goals and become affluent. Striving, as a way of life, appears to be confirmed.

Figure 3:4 Roots of Major Twentieth-century Cohorts

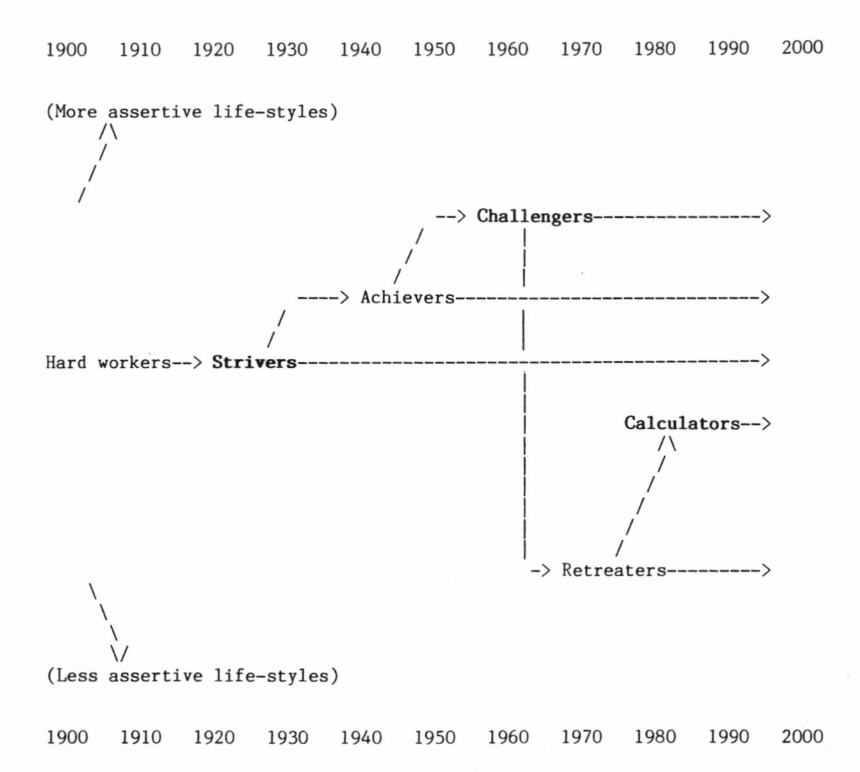

Which of the two emphases dominates in the framework of an individual Striver is often determined by age. Older and less affluent Strivers are more likely now to reflect their hard-work, constant-striving origins; later and more affluent Strivers tend to be less intense and follow a life-style more typical of persons who enjoy the benefits of achievement. Yet even such "Achievers" (these more successful Strivers) continue to approach life with intensity; many work hard at recreation, for example. Figure 3:4 shows the variety that has emerged among Strivers by including lines for both Strivers and the later-emerging Achievers. As the pattern of the lines indicates, not all Strivers become Achievers; many continue to exhibit a basic, hard-worker life-style. But all Achievers carry basic Striver feelings and attitudes within their frameworks.

Challengers' reflective framework, like that of the Strivers, is a composite. But whereas most Strivers see the basic attitudes of their early shaping confirmed during their adult years, most Challengers do not.

Challengers begin as children in the affluent world the Strivers achieved. They are privileged at the start. During their childhood years,

Challengers' parents often seek to instill them with the value of hard work, but Challengers, seeing abundance all around them, question the necessity of a lifetime of hard work and constant striving. The unusual affluence of the post-World War II era appears as a given to Strivers and, because it turns out to be temporary, becomes a major initial, destabilizing experience for them. Challengers as a cohort enter the larger society with two unrealistic beliefs: (1) I can do (have, achieve) whatever I want; (2) so can everybody else.

But frustrations soon appear. Challengers are radically destabilized a second time, in this instance by unanticipated psychological, social, and economic limits that take shape in the midst of their abundant experiences and visions. As a result of these successive destabilizations, most Challengers presently function through a contradictory framework: composed of a continuing, and sometimes unrealistically, high estimate of human possibilities, on the one hand, and repeated experiences with frustrating reverses, on the other. Out of frustration, many Challengers have scaled down their original visions for themselves and society. I call those who have so revised their frameworks and their lives "Retreaters."[10]

As is the case with Strivers, some Challengers presently hold more to earlier, "challenging" visions, whereas others, especially those who have personally faced considerable reverses, function more as "Retreaters." But, unlike Strivers, Challengers' more recent experiences contrast sharply with their earlier experiences. Again, as with the Strivers, lines are plotted in the diagram both for those who follow the original Challenger pattern and for those who become Retreaters. Retreaters, however, have been dropped below the center of the figure, to indicate the sense of frustration and confinement many now describe.

Calculators begin in the midst of the Challengers' experience of retreat. They see the corporate and individual illusions and consequences of challenging, from deep hurts that conclude permissive marriages and blown minds that follow in the aftermath of drug experimentation to the economic difficulties many Challengers now face in middle age.

The pervasiveness of the Calculators' more conservative approach to life is apparent in a recent study of the nation's college students conducted by the University of California at Los Angeles. The contrast between the students of today and those who were students during the Challengers' prime time is staggering. Between 1967 and 1982 the percentage of undergraduate students pursuing degrees in literature, history, and foreign languages dropped by two thirds. Nearly 24 percent of all current college students intend to major in business—two and one half times as many as in 1972. "This incredible preoccupation with getting a job and making a living—at the expense of developing a talent, saving the world and whatever else kids used to dream of—is a startling diversion of our talent stream and will have profound implications for our future as a civilization."[11]

Thus, as they prepare to venture into the larger society, Calculators believe that they need to equip themselves to compete well. Their decisions about which educational and career options to pursue are based on sober estimates of the consequences of the options they see. Obviously their recent emergence as a cohort makes Calculators' complete framework difficult to envision. But the basic outline of their approach to life seems clear.

I realize that any attempt to categorize people is bound to appear, to some degree, both arbitrary and forced. It will describe the ways some individuals function more adequately than it describes others, probably because some people are more consistent and predictable than others. I am also aware that minority groups pass through their own, unique experiences in each age, some of which are very different from the majority experiences I have outlined.[12] Throughout their lives some people conform largely to patterns defined during their early socialization, for example, those who live in self-segregating ethnic and social groups and those who remain within traditional (often rural) communities only slightly affected by social change. Finally, some people are more independent individuals, who disassociate themselves more readily from the groups within which they are socialized or, in response to changing conditions, easily adopt new patterns of living and believing.

But over the years I have encountered relatively few persons who seem able (willing?) to adapt their frameworks repeatedly to include perspectives that differ radically from those they adopted during the years of their initial acculturation. In his wide-ranging study of contemporary American life-styles, *The Nine American Lifestyles,* Arnold Mitchell calls such people "Integrateds" and finds that they compose *only 2 percent* of the U.S. population.[13] My own research agrees. Throughout their lives most people continue to be influenced to a great extent, many to be dominated, by the reflective elements in their frameworks. When new times call for changes in behavior and attitudes that violate the basic framework shaped during their childhood, or a prime time, such changes seem abnormal, and the situation that calls for them, temporary to most people. Thus, Strivers adjust to their children who, as adults, decide to "live together" but don't see them as "normal" until they marry. Challengers adjust to economic reverses and a scaling down of social justice goals but believe they should not have to. Many continue to hunger for a return of abundance and look forward to a time when all can share in that abundance, despite evidence that neither the earth nor human systems have the capacity to deliver what they long for.

The sheer variety of options for living and believing now available is novel and challenging in itself. Fifty years ago most people expected to fit their lives into well-defined and readily-available patterns laid down by those who preceded them. Now, radical social change has left us with varied experiences and perceptions of space and time. Deciding what to believe and how to live is no simple task today, either for us as individuals or, as the next chapter shows, for churches that are called on to guide and support us.

CHAPTER FOUR

Churches Caught in Space and Time

Quite frequently I hear church members lament the present restriction of the church's influence in society. When we consider the effects of massive social change like that I have analyzed in the first three chapters, such complaints are understandable. Although some people probably applaud and others regret this growing restriction of the church's direct influence, hardly anyone fails to acknowledge the constraints.

Our everyday experience is full of reminders. For example, although some among us struggle intently to "put God back in the schools," most of us are clear from the opinions of the courts that *prescribed* prayer in public schools violates the spirit as well as the letter of our Constitution. (Hence the movement to amend the Constitution.) Few among us believe that we can look forward to a future that will include religious instruction in a public school like that I helped to conduct in the central school during my years as pastor in a rural village. And just about every attempt to provide tax support for nonreligious programs in parochial schools is quickly declared unconstitutional by the courts. The use of public funds to support even nonreligious education in parochial schools is seldom permitted, just as the church is excluded from direct influence in the public schools.

The church is excluded from other segments as well. Attempts by religious groups to retain "blue laws" that prevent stores from doing business on Sunday are most often futile. Nor do individuals have the right to refuse to report to work on a day that is their sabbath. Like all groups and organizations in our society, churches are now expected to restrict their activities to their own segment.

One result of this progressive restriction is that more and more people find it difficult to envision how the church can in any way effectively influence life in segments other than its own. When I conduct church-strategy consultations I can often help people to clarify the dilemma (and transition) that now frustrates them by showing two slides in succession.

The first slide is a picture of a dirt road with a small white church located to one side. As they see this slide, most people can easily talk about how and why the church is present to all of life in the world they envision.

The other slide shows three intertwining tiers of an interstate highway. I ask the same groups to describe how the church relates to the world they associate with the second slide. Few people can look at the slide and describe how the local church is *directly* present to the segmented world it calls to mind.

It seldom is. Some people can describe how local church *members* might be present, but most are unable to describe how the local church, *as a unit,* is effectively present. What was once seen as typical has now become unusual. The local church is now perceived as spaced out and spaced in.

The Separated Church

The progressive distancing of the church from so much of our living is a critical problem for those of us who are concerned to live as Christians in all of life. Once we leave the gathered Christian community, we seem very much on our own. We hunger for the support, the insight, the resources, and the presence the church once provided, especially those of us who have lived in a time and in places where a local church was directly connected to much of life.

As I mentioned earlier, even in my three decades of ministry I remember such good times and places. In the years leading up to my pastor-friend's unnerving encounter with his nuclear physicist-parishioner (the one who quit his job when he saw himself contributing to killing), I carried on a day-to-day ministry, supporting church members who were effectively relating their faith to their activities in government, work, and community life.

For example, I recall many afternoons spent with Mel, the county probation officer, searching with him for God's direction as he made his rounds to visit his charges. Together we worked through the tension he often felt between his responsibility to keep his charges accountable on the one hand and his concern to share the redemptive reality of God on the other. When he and I gathered with other members of the support group in our local church, most of them understood firsthand the struggles he shared and were able to offer continuing, vital support.

On some occasions the local police officer would ask me to go with him as he responded to calls to intervene in domestic squabbles that had or threatened to escalate into violence. I especially remember one evening when he asked me to enter an apartment *first* where a husband was threatening to shoot his wife—and anybody else who tried to intervene. He sought to soothe my anxiety by saying, "He won't shoot you; you're a *minister!*" Fortunately he was correct. I was often impressed with his concern to do his duty as a Christian as much as his duty as an officer of the law. Again, we all knew him and cared for him.

But as the years passed, such links between the local church and other segments of life became more difficult to maintain. I first noticed the difficulty as we attempted to minister with the growing number of commuters in my parishes. Their work worlds were so varied and remote from the rest of us who gathered in the church that we were often not able to appreciate their dilemmas. It was similar to another dilemma we felt during the sixties and seventies: increasingly our children left the community to join an alien world and culture, which many of us find difficult even to appreciate, let alone enter.

But what has most frustrated me and many others who are concerned to relate faith to all of life is the growing sense of powerlessness we experience when we seek to live out our faith in those segments of life now located largely beyond the local church's *direct* influence. Let me share an incident that may help to point up the nature of the dilemma.

The incident occurred in a group of local church members concerned to link their faith to work and community life. On this particular evening a member—we will call her "Susan" (not her real name)—shared with the group her inability to make a decision in a situation that confronted her at work that day. At the time she held a job by political appointment in the finance department of a state legislature. She told us that a man had appeared in the office that morning asking for his paycheck. She went to the file, looked under his name, found an authorization, and then went to the safe, where she discovered a check written to him for several thousand dollars. Thinking there must be some error, she consulted her supervisor, who assured her there was none. So, she asked the man to sign for his check and then handed it to him. He thanked her and left.

But as the day went on, in spite of her supervisor's reassurance, Susan continued to be troubled by the incident. So she investigated. By the end of the day she discovered that the man to whom she had given the check had done some "favors" for a high-ranking official in the legislature and in return for those favors was being compensated for a "no-show" job, a job that existed only as a title. He had really done no work.

Susan was devastated by what she discovered and by what she had done. "I paid him off!" she confessed to the church group that evening. "You are my support group; help me decide what to do!"

We were baffled.

Susan reflected on the options as she saw them:

> I could go in there tomorrow and confront everybody. I've seen what happens to people who do that sort of thing; I'd be out of a job by lunchtime!
>
> Or I could keep quiet and seek ways to bring more integrity to the department. That *might* be effective; it would probably be a long time before I saw any results. But I don't know whether I can live with myself, if I keep quiet about what I know.

We struggled to be helpful to Susan that evening and in the weeks that followed, as she sought ways to live as a responsible Christian at her workplace. The dilemma she confessed encouraged similar sharing by others in the group. For more than a year we attempted to support one another's efforts. But as the months went by we had a growing sense of the group's ineffectiveness. Members shared less and less, and the group became more and more superficial. Finally, we stopped meeting. As far as faith and life at work were concerned, we could neither get it all together nor keep it all together.

Friends making similar efforts with groups in their congregations often report similar experiences. Looking closely at our attempts, I see that many of us begin these efforts to relate our faith directly to all of life in response to what we identify as a necessary, as well as hopeful, vision. The content of that vision is expressed well by the report of the section focused on the laity at the Evanston meeting of the World Council of Churches:

> The real battles of the faith today are being fought in factories, shops, offices and farms, in political parties and government agencies, in countless homes, in the press, radio and television, in the relationship of nations. Very often it is said that the Church should "go into these spheres"; but the fact is, the Church is already in these spheres in the persons of its laity.[1]

Hopeful words, but in reality the program called for proves difficult to implement. Few among us envision the dilemmas that will befall us as we find ourselves alone and quite unable to identify a clearly "Christian" course of action—other than to withdraw or take a stand and be expelled. And there is something unsettling about the thought that the only way for Christians to remain Christians is to withdraw or be expelled from segments beyond the church.

In a society disintegrated into semiautonomous realms, more and more church members encounter predicaments similar to Susan's. It becomes increasingly difficult to retain them as members of groups committed to relate faith to life beyond the church. Nor is it easy to enlist other lay persons in ministries that repeatedly involve them in dilemmas that seem to have no clear-cut resolution, and that in the end they usually have to resolve on their own.

Frankly, I find that most ministers and lay persons today discuss the relation of faith to *daily* life largely in moralistic and general terms. With developing segmentation, those of us who are clergy have less information about the specific decisions our parishioners face. And living with the distancing of the church from life (recall the slide of the interstate highways), many (most?) of us who are lay persons feel that the church is remote from much (most?) of our daily living. What is true of those segments where the links are the most difficult to effect—like work and government and school—soon spreads to other areas of our lives as well. Our lifeways at home and at leisure also become more distant from our church experience.

As time passes and our living in other segments becomes alien to our church experience, we feel direct connections are less possible. And desirable. Recalling the struggles of people like the nuclear physicist and Susan, and uncertain about whether the way we live at home and at play would stand the scrutiny of the church, we may not even want the church to relate directly to our daily living. Of necessity we have made compromises. Perhaps many of us have our own hidden "Watergates" that would more than embarrass us if they should come to light.

Many of us now feel the physicist's dilemma in our own lives; it would now be costly for us to "get it all together." We have built a framework of survival within which we have learned not to look for connections among the segments. As with Bobby's blue auras, we have decided that the connections are impossible. Or not desirable. So we have stopped seeing them.

Responses to Segmentation

I do not mean to imply that the church has done nothing effective to respond to social change. Also, I realize that "effective" is a matter of judgment, and that many Christians do find nurture and support from the resources the church now provides. But how well do the available efforts enable Christians of various ages and cohorts to live faithfully in our *segmented* society? Let us consider several approaches.

Advocates of one approach believe that the major need is to equip us *personally* with the *individual* resources we need to survive the demands of living in today's world. But, although much of what they suggest is helpful, they seldom take into account the *structural dilemmas* most of us confront as we move through a segmented world.

Others attempt to help us solve the difficulty of linking the church to other segments by encouraging us to identify and then *live with the options that are possible within each situation* in which we find ourselves. Their suggestions also are helpful but seem to assume too readily that all of us can both discover within each segment what to do and then find the faith resources to follow through on what we decide.

A third group hopes to make the church more effective by *strengthening and enlarging the church segment, especially at the denominational and ecumenical levels, thereby increasing the church's ability to influence society as a whole*. A stronger church *can* offer more effective support and challenge, especially at national and international levels. But in their zeal to enlist the support of church members to address whatever they feel is the critical agenda, those who seek to scale up the church often seem to overestimate our ability to respond to the dilemmas we face as individuals in our daily living.

Advocates of a fourth approach believe that *what we do within the* local *church and our own* individual *lives is by far most important*—and easiest to control; we are better off when we concentrate on the local church and our local, individual living. The strength of their discipline may be impressive, but proponents of this fourth approach seem to assume too readily that we can simply withdraw to avoid the conflicting demands of living that face us in the world beyond the church's direct influence.

In summary, the options readily available to Christians suggest either an individual, situational, organizational, or sectarian response to segmentation. Although Christians committed to each strategy are obviously nurtured, none of these approaches seem to describe adequately how a distanced local church can provide us with the resources we need to live as Christians within a segmented society. Consider, first, those who focus on providing resources to individuals.

Each year I pass many hours in airports waiting for airplanes that will take me to and from meetings and consultations. Quite frequently, while waiting for my flight to depart, I pass the time looking over the books offered for sale to travelers—especially the books with a religious focus.

The books of such popular ministers as Norman Vincent Peale, Billy Graham, and Robert Schuller are usually prominently displayed. A little lower down on the rack are the works of people who are judged to have a more specific or limited appeal, like Thomas Merton, Kahlil Gibran, and Alan Watts. The more complete collections include books describing the techniques and benefits of various Eastern religions, as well as suggestions from those with more closely Christian roots, like Laurence Le Shan *(How to Meditate)*.

What is not surprising, but might be, had we not come to take the affinity for granted, is the location nearby of popular self-help books that are not religous at all, but apparently speak to the same needs and concerns as the religious books do. I am thinking of books that promise to reveal the life-changing secrets of techniques like EST, and others with intriguing titles like *Winning Through Intimidation*. There is nearly always a generous offering of books based on some of the current, popular psychologies, like gestalt or transactional analysis (TA). Examples include the TA-based *Born to Win* by Muriel James, Thomas Harris' classic *I'm O.K., You're O.K.,* and the gestalt therapy books of Fritz Perls.

What stands out over three decades is the consistency of the offerings. Although new authors may appear, the old standbys remain. As time passes, however, the emphasis is less on the help that God can provide and more on self-help. Over the years Dr. Peale's popularity has increasingly been challenged by the Eric Bernes and Leo Buscaglias. Even as the focus shifts, the promise remains constant: "With the help of ______ you can make it."

For many Americans today, religion has become an individual, "do-it-yourself" affair. While for generations some Americans have lacked confidence in the church, the apparent inability of local churches today to relate to most areas of life encourages even more people to think they must make their own way. The books on the shelves of popular bookstores represent a cafeteria of options designed to assist those who believe they have to plan their own faith journeys. The books seem to say, especially to those most on the move from segment to segment, "Let us help you develop a customized 'religion.' "

I call this first response to segmentation the *individual* response. Although it may have been more popular a few years ago, it is still a widespread approach today, as the continuing popularity of books like those I have been describing testifies. Their sales in airports and other places frequented by "busy" people may offer some clues about the kind of person to whom this approach appeals. The selection of books in airports is designed to appeal to those most "on the move." Such mobile people are among those *least* likely to participate in local churches because they especially don't find such participation helpful. And, as noted in chapter 2, they are likely to be persons to whom local churches seem isolated and remote.

The large sales of religious and semireligious self-help books that appeal to mobile and marginally churched or unchurched individuals may help to explain why there has been little or no decrease in religious belief or concern in the past few years in the face of a significant decline in church participation. Speaking from a local church perspective, a friend once described these middle-class, affluent, and mobile people as the "up-and-outs." Along with the sixties generation as a whole (whose approach to believing will be of major concern in chapter 5), they may account for the largest proportion of dropouts from the church. For nearly two decades my own research on church participation has provided clear indications that upwardly mobile people move away from participation in local churches. I have consistently seen congregations that draw their participants from among those who hold higher-status jobs, earn higher incomes, and contain a large proportion of college graduates lose the most members.[2]

My findings are supported by other research covering the same period of years.[3] These studies consistently show those denominations that traditionally appeal most to the same higher-status people losing the most members. Especially from 1965 onward, Episcopalians, Unitarian-Universalists, and Presbyterians experienced greater percentage losses than did Roman Catholics, Southern Baptists, and the various sects (many of which gained members).

A major work that further clarifies the types of persons who do and do not find participating in a local congregation helpful is Wade Clark Roof's *Community and Commitment*.[4] Taking a cue from Robert K. Merton,[5] Roof studies the commitment patterns of those he identifies as "locals" and "cosmopolitans." Locals are people who focus their living in a restricted area; usually they originated in or are primarily oriented to the local community where they now reside. Cosmopolitans are the opposite: they move regularly from place to place and daily from segment to segment.

As we might expect, Roof finds that locals tend to be more active and committed to local congregations; what the local church stands for is both more plausible and more effective in their experience. He specifically reports that 65 percent of the locals in his study attend worship services nearly every week compared with 34 percent of the cosmopolitans; 46 percent of the locals are highly involved in church activities compared with 23 percent of the cosmopolitans; 52 percent of the locals have a large number of friends in the congregation where they are members compared with only 29 percent of the cosmopolitans.[6]

A consistent pattern emerges from all this research: those most affected by the segmentation of society are also most likely to attempt an individual and personal approach to religion and are least likely to become or remain active in local congregations. A variety of literature and "services" has emerged to meet the needs of such people. These resources focus on instrumental approaches to religion and other personal growth techniques. They offer suggestions for individuals seeking to build personal resources that will enable them to stand up to the challenges of life in a segmented world. They emphasize the ability of a powerful, personal faith and the techniques of ______ to withstand the challenges of everyday life. The message is consistent: "Whatever your difficulties, God or ______ will help you to surmount them!"

When we read one of these books, or watch an inspiring church service alone in front of a television set, the simple message presented may seem convincing and sufficient. It definitely seems more plausible when we are safe at home than it does in a church group where someone has just shared a story like Susan's and asked us to help her decide what to do tomorrow when she returns to the same office where she was trapped in an illegal scheme. In that group it becomes evident that the problem is not simply stress, but *conflict*. A common flaw of self-help programs now becomes apparent. Strengthening our individual, personal resources can help us to live with our stress, but that does not necessarily enable us to resolve the structural conflicts that emerge as we move among autonomous segments.

A second response to segmentation does take into consideration the structural dilemmas of unconnected living and the inability of the church to relate *directly* to much of life. Proponents of this approach suggest that *our faith and our ethical decisions must be as segmented as our living.* Realistically, we can decide what to do in each situation in which we find ourselves only on the basis of the options that are possible *within that situation*. I call this style of response the *situational* approach. It was first promoted almost simultaneously in the early 1960s by two theologians living on opposite sides of the Atlantic Ocean.

Bishop John Robinson's *Honest to God* appeared in 1963 and Joseph Fletcher's *Situation Ethics*, in 1966 (although the kernel of Fletcher's thinking appeared much earlier, in an article published in 1959).[7] Each book created quite a stir; Robinson especially was called both a saint and a heretic, depending on the reader's viewpoint. His book was significant especially because it was written for and read by lay persons as much as clergy, and because it attracted the attention of many who were no longer active in the church.

In *Honest to God* the bishop seeks to provide "honest" and workable descriptions of God and the Christian life in terms that make sense and are functional within contemporary culture and society. In the light of contemporary cosmology he attempts to conceptualize where God "is" ("up there or out there?") and, with a good deal of help from the writing of Paul Tillich, finally describes God as a "depth at the centre of life."[8]

Robinson then turns to ethics and, with suggestions drawn mostly from Fletcher, concludes that the church can no longer define an *overarching* ethical system. Under the old system " 'the clear teaching of our Lord' is taken to mean that Jesus laid down certain precepts which were universally binding. Certain things were always right, and other things were always wrong—for all men [and women] everywhere."[9]

Bishop Robinson then goes on to advocate an alternative approach, beginning with a quote from Fletcher's article. "Christian ethics is not a scheme of codified conduct. It is a purposive effort to relate love to a world of relativities through a casuistry obedient to love."[10] To which the bishop adds his own comment: "It is a radical 'ethic of the situation,' with nothing prescribed—except love."[11] What one should or should not do, therefore, cannot be defined apart from people and the situation in which a decision presents itself. The overarching constraint that links all of life together is obedience to love.

The approach seems tailor-made for those who must live in a segmented world. It offers individuals the freedom to define their Christian responsibility in terms of what is possible and what they personally feel called to do in each particular setting. It recognizes that what may be possible in one setting is not possible in another; likewise, what may be possible for different people within the same setting may be quite different. Why, then, did it fade from popularity so quickly? There are several reasons.

First, it takes a capable and strong person to identify and weigh the options in situations where the alternatives are not *obviously* or categorically good and bad. Many people do not have the wherewithal to make such decisions independently and then move on to live independently with the outcomes of their decisions. The strength of the nuclear physicist who decided to quit his job rather than contribute to the development of missile-carrying submarines is exceptional.

Second, situation ethics underestimates the power of those in authority in bureaucratically organized segments. The only unambiguous power that Susan had in her situation was to leave her job. Her decision to stay committed her to live in a continuing ambiguity where she had no way of knowing whether her efforts at change would have any effect.

Third, the relativity of situation ethics proves too threatening, psychologically, to many church members. They prefer to hold on to a framework that suggests Christians can choose according to an absolute, all-encompassing, ethical scheme, even though, when pressed, most are hard put to describe specifically how such a scheme can function in the lives of those who live in a segmented society. When faced with a dilemma like Susan's, they tend to see the Christian as one who either always withdraws or stands up to her or his principles and is fired.

Finally, especially since the 1960s, the reality and possibility of God's effective presence in all of life (theologically known as the doctrine of Providence) has become questionable for more and more people. The so-called God-is-dead theologians (who, as we shall see in the next section also emerged during the 1960s) symbolize a growing theological uncertainty that redefinitions by theologians like Bishop Robinson and his successors have not been able to quell. Such questioning makes situation ethics difficult to act out. It is even more difficult to "keep the faith" in tough situations when the faith itself is ambiguous.

Advocates of a third response to segmentation seek to strengthen and enlarge the church, especially at the denominational and ecumenical levels. I call their varied efforts the *organizational* response to segmentation.

To some degree, these attempts follow a pattern similar to the scale-up we have seen in government and corporate structures.[12] Supporters of the approach may encourage such a scaling up to increase the ability of the church to challenge the centralized power of other segments.

Actually, scale-up in the church has been developing for at least 150 years. Current efforts build on a trend that began with the evangelical "awakening" movements of the early nineteenth century. The trend continued in the abolitionist and foreign mission movements that emerged during the rest of that century and has been visible in the ecumenical movement and, most recently, the corporate and highly bureaucratic denominational structures of the twentieth century.[13]

Once this transition is complete, local congregations discover they also have been transformed: from associations defined primarily from within their own communities into subunits of national denominations. They are now defined at least as much by the connections they have beyond their communities as by the roles they play within their communities.

Current support for the trend toward scale-up and centralization within the church is understandable and often justified. We have already seen how church members who seek to act out their faith in other segments of life can be frustrated by the autonomous and centralized control exercised within these segments. For example, how many individual church members can *directly* challenge global injustice? Repeated frustration when they seek to be faithful in segments beyond the church's control may encourage church members to support a movement to enhance the corporate power of the church. Only national church leaders have *direct* access to heads of corporations and governments who have power to change corporate policies. In our world today it seems necessary for the church to organize and scale-up to be in a challenging position. At its best, a scaled-up church can be a formidable force for good; for example, it can mobilize and coordinate resources to oppose injustice.

Yet there are some subtle tendencies in such a scaling up that give cause for concern. When the "important" agenda is again and again defined within a national or international context, a *direct* response is possible only for a minority. Nearly everyone can participate *in*directly (sending money, telegrams, letters, etc.), but only a few are able to break away regularly from their responsibilities of work, parenting, community ministry, etc. to travel to Central America, or whatever other scene is currently the focus of concern.

By inference (usually not by intention) the responsibilities of "ordinary" Christians appear to be discounted. Their daily experiences of oppression at work may be just as painful as those described in the denomination's literature; their care of a foster child just as significant a ministry; their volunteer work in a local literacy program just as essential. But the focus and thrust of denominational attention seems to indicate that major concerns are to be found mostly, or only, "at the top."

Rank and file church members are encouraged into a support role. Their commitment is solicited most often for the denominational program. Moreover, denominational officials (whose major agendas are usually denominational agendas) tend to praise those congregations whose members are willing to contribute a large portion of their resources to support denominational efforts. In the face of such an emphasis it is easy for church members to gain the impression that they are valued mostly for the support they provide their denomination.

Ordained ministers also often support the upwardly focused denominational system. They are usually more familiar with the goals and programs of the denomination than anyone else in their congregations. The minister's personal perspective tends to be nonlocal anyway. Most local pastors today are only temporary residents of the communities in which they minister. In terms of acculturation, they are much more like "cosmopolitans," with their global perspectives and concerns, than they are like "locals," who focus their concern and energy on the community in which they live.

Clergy also have a personal investment in mobilizing support for their denomination's programs. Denominational officials usually play a major role in ministers' placement and advancement. It behooves ministers to impress them with their loyalty to the denomination and its causes. A minister's future is not so much bound up with the present congregation he or she serves as with the denomination to which the minister belongs.

Making the support of local church members in their local ministries primary involves genuine risks for clergy. A minister who invests heavily in a local congregation, who sees the ministries of its members as primary, contradicts the mores, needs, momentum, and power of the denomination to which he or she belongs. All of which jeopardizes his or her career advancement.

Thus, the scaled-up, corporate church may, on the one hand, provide a powerful challenge to other power structures in a scaled-up, corporate society. On the other hand, such an upward focus involves only a minority *directly* and may leave the majority of local church members wondering how they can serve God in their daily lives.

The fourth response to segmentation I call the *sectarian* approach, even though it involves some congregations that are not "sectarian" in the strict definition of the word. I use the word sectarian to describe a way of responding, not to define a congregation's history or current affiliation.

A growing number of congregations encourage their members to respond to the difficulties of living in a segmented society *by making the church segment the primary segment*. Those who choose this response give the church primary time and attention and in return expect the church to provide them with the resources and protection they need to live as Christians. Moving in the opposite direction from those who seek to scale up the church, their primary concern is the role and Christian action of each individual church member. In fact, the present popularity of the segmented approach among congregations within mainstream denominations is, in part, a reaction against the centralizing of power, resources, and concern in these scaled-up denominations.

The growing number of conservative and often independent, or only weakly linked, congregations over the past two or three decades testifies to the increasing popularity of the sectarian aproach. During recent years, as I have driven past the increasing number of church signs that read something like "Calvary Bible Church—an Independent, Fundamental, Bible-Believing Fellowship," I have seen more and more visual evidence of the growth of such independent congregations.

Set apart is a central concern of these churches. Members of each congregation usually carry on many, if not most, of the activities of life with one another; they concentrate their living within the church segment. For example, often, even on a weekday, I see children present at a church building, indicating that that congregation sponsors a Christian day school. The proliferation of Christian schools during the past two decades is startling: from about 1,000 in 1965 to nearly 13,000 in 1985.[14]

These congregations may also provide such other services as Christian bookstores, Christian counseling centers, Christian day care. One group even supports a campground, advertising on their sign that they offer " a Christian camping experience." Whatever the congregation supports, each activity is designed to promote a well-defined, Christian point of view. (The day-care program includes Christian instruction; the bookstore selection tends to be limited to those books in harmony with the church's viewpoint.)

Members of these congregations accept the fact that the society in which we live has become segmented. They openly regret the fact that most segments are now "secular" and beyond the church's control (although not beyond the influence of individual Christians, some of whom, as accepted spokespersons for their viewpoint, are expected to exert national and international influence). Faced by the loss of that protective, social accountability the church could provide when it was physically present to all of life, they believe the safest course now is to concentrate as much of life as possible in the church segment.

Participants in these churches are encouraged to socialize mostly with other members of their congregation and sometimes are discouraged from socializing with nonmembers. The ten-year-old son of one of my neighbors says that he is not permitted to play with a boy who lives up the road from him. "They can't play with anybody who doesn't go to their church." Other family members are similarly encouraged to carry on their social activities within the congregation.

In recent years a growing number of these independent congregations have formed coalitions with congregations composed of like-minded people.

Such networks provide denominationlike support services to the congregations. For example, a young man and woman about to be married in a local, independent church were required to attend a regional, premarriage conference, where they were instructed about the proper roles "Christian" husbands and wives are supposed to assume. On the couple's return the wife-to-be reported that she now understood why she would promise to "obey" her husband in the wedding ceremony.

Linkages to like-minded congregations also provide opportunities to work jointly at efforts to promote legislation designed to bring the society, as a whole, in line with moral viewpoints espoused by member congregations (e.g., the pro-life movement, joint efforts to oppose gay/lesbian rights legislation, the effort to secure a constitutional amendment that will permit prayer in the public schools).

As with all sectarian-type movements, insofar as daily experience tends to increase the sense of support individuals receive from the group, it also increases their loyalty and dependence on the group. Members tend to spend most of their time with other members of their church. Other church members, and especially leaders of the congregation, are viewed as the most reliable sources of information. Insofar as the church member is socialized by the group, he or she tends to accept the cultural framework of the group and to reinforce in his or her experience the world view of the congregation. That world view then works in the individual's experience to the extent that he or she is able to concentrate life in the church segment and order life beyond that segment in accordance with the norms of the church. It may also serve as some protection when outsiders who are aware of the church's norms refrain from placing church members in predicaments that might be difficult for them (e.g., social settings in which liquor is served).

This sectarian, concentrate-life-in-church solution to living in a segmented society often has limited appeal or utility among those who spend most of their time in segments where church norms do not or cannot dominate—which, for most of us, currently includes a great deal of life. In these realms individual autonomy is limited. People like Susan, who live within ambiguous situations where they exercise limited control, are the least able to keep to the typically rigid norms of these generally conservative churches, unless they are willing to deny the reality of what they see and the restrictions imposed on what they can do.

The current popularity of the conservative churches stems not only from the fact that they are clearly in the "religion business" (as the author of one of the most popular books describing these churches has suggested[15]), but also from their concentration on the church segment in which the traditional approach to religion still works. Especially in rural areas, where the traditional community is more intact, the separatist attitude prevails among sectarian and mainstream congregations alike. The attitude is also popular among those who are economically independent and powerful enough to exercise control throughout most of their lives. Thus, it is not surprising to find those at higher levels in government and corporate structures espousing a sectarian viewpoint.

The limits of such a restrictive approach to resolving the dilemmas of living in a segmented world confront most of us in the daily compromises we face in segments beyond the church's control. It *is* uncomfortable to recognize that most of our lives are carried on beyond the church's protective web. Three or four years ago I attempted to challenge what seemed to me to be the overly restrictive lifeway of a congregation that employed me as a planning consultant. One woman, who functioned as a spokesperson for the group, was particularly articulate during the breakfast meeting that concluded the consultation. She spoke of the importance of the protection their church program provides, especially for her own children and young people. She touted the wholesome influence not only of the congregation's Sunday school, but also of their Christian grade school. She planned to send her children to a Christian high school. She told us she was happy that they could go to a local roller rink for recreation because she knew it was owned and operated by a Christian.

At the close of this early breakfast meeting a man who also had attended gave me a ride to the airport. It would be on his way, he told me, because he works for a large electronics firm at an office located near the airport. As we rode along I asked him what he thought of the meeting. He was silent for a time. Then he replied, with an obvious reference to the woman who had dominated the conversation: "I've been wondering how in hell she will find a Christian computer company where her kids can work when they grow up!"

I couldn't describe the dilemma better. Few of us can really avoid the present world. And the new shape of that world undermines our church structures and challenges our traditional Christian frameworks more deeply than the available church options recognize.

When There Is No Church to Go Back To

The young man who gave me a ride to the airport is a Challenger. Like many Challengers, he is frustrated by the inability of his church to accept and help him address the changing world in which he and his friends live. The persistent woman is a Striver. The church in its traditional form still "works" for her, to some degree because she spends most of her time in church, home, and family segments, where she can exercise quite a bit of control over her living. Like many of those who hold power and exercise leadership in local churches today, this woman doesn't want her protected living and believing invaded by the world that is.

Such a defensive response to social change is common today, both in society at large and among church members in particular. As we have seen repeatedly in this book, most of us update our frameworks and change the patterns of our living only as we are forced to do so. For example, the last U.S. Census to show a majority of Americans living in nonmetropolitan areas was taken in 1910. Not since the decade that included World War I have a majority of Americans *geographically* had rural roots. Yet, as James

Oliver Robinson demonstrates in *American Myth, American Reality,* it was not until the middle of this century or later that many of us began to face up to the implications of urbanization in our frameworks.[16]

Robinson suggests that we Americans have long sought to protect ourselves against the realities of social change by clinging to the myth that we still have a rural home to which we can return to recover our bearings. This rural home represents the "real" world to which we can return whenever we need to rediscover who we really are. Quoting from Peter Schrag's *The End of the American Future,* Robinson points out that even into the 1970s, many of us held on to the belief that every American was

> in reality "a small-town boy come home," and that the city, its life, and its attitudes "was something you put on, but Main Street was something you remained forever." . . .
>
> "Every time you flew across the country or looked at the ads on television, the vision returned: Down there was the real America, on the wheat fields of Kansas, in the small crossroads towns with their friendly Mutual of Omaha insurance agent, in the shopping centers where the farmers congregated on Saturday afternoon and the women came to have their hair set . . . and men bought tires and where things always went better with Coke."[17]

The traditional church, with its cohesive moral influence, also dependably "back there," was part of this reassuring picture. Where and however far we might stray most of us believed, like those suburban Strivers with whom I began my ministry in the mid-1950s, that we could always return "home" to find our bearings again.

But such attempts to evade reality by maintaining social and religious myths in the face of social change are ultimately costly. When change finally breaks through into our frameworks to face us as unavoidable reality, our frameworks are severely shaken, if not shattered, along with the myths on which they depend. Like the Striver woman seeking to protect her children within Christian schools and Christian roller rinks, we know the only way we might protect our way of living and believing is to confine ourselves to protected spaces.

But protected spaces are increasingly hard to find, and harder yet to maintain. As Peter Schrag suggests, most of us are now face to face with a scarey truth: we have "lost the country" and with that loss the possibility of going back to the old hometown and the old-time religion to recover a sense of direction and basic values that will show us how we can and should live today. Many of the approaches to living suggested by the old-time values and religion don't work in the world in which we have to live because, as we have seen, that world is *structurally* different. Once we enter the era of the Challengers, if we maintain the old, traditional framework, we soon discover we are handicapped. When we hold to that obsolete framework, we soon discover we are adrift in a world for which we lack not only an adequate ethic,[18] but also an adequate faith. The difficulty of knowing what to do is now matched by the difficulty of knowing how to believe.

In the mid-1960s, before the undermining effects of social change were generally apparent, several radical theologians began to describe the growing difficulty of believing in God (as most Christians have conceived of God) in contemporary, urbanized culture. A few even suggested that social change had progressed far enough to render the very existence of God questionable. Such radical theology created quite a stir; even *Time* magazine ran a cover story under the headline "Is God Dead?"[19]

From the way they reacted to the theological news, the prospect of God's death seemed ludicrous, if not preposterous, to most of the church members with whom I talked. Perhaps the term dead overstated the problem. Yet their eyes often revealed an uncertainty that their loud protesting failed to cover up, especially the Strivers among them, whose frameworks were most undermined by the recent social and cultural changes that precipitated the theologians' questions. Although most Challengers were not so obviously displaced, given their socialization into an already-segmented world, many were, and still are, having even more difficulty seeing how God can be present to all of life. Few Challengers, for example, have a nostalgic framework (myth of the indestructible country) into which they can withdraw when the stresses of change threaten to overwhelm them.

The more I listened to the questions people shared with me in various study and prayer and ministry groups, the more it became apparent to me that quite a few of them were losing (or were unable to develop) the capacity to envision how God could relate *effectively* to some of the segments in which they lived. To be honest, so was I.

I suspect that people with whom I share her story are struck so profoundly by Susan's dilemma (once she discovers she has cooperated in an illegal scheme at the office) not simply because she is powerless to act effectively at her workplace; they also wonder how God can act there. If God is contained, or constrained, *anywhere,* then is God still God? The God-is-dead theologians struck a surprisingly resonant chord of anxiety among many who didn't take the time to read, much less critique, their arguments. Those vibrations still resonate.

Only with great difficulty can we maintain a framework that is repeatedly contradicted by the experiences of our daily living. The more our activities contradict our framework, the more difficult it becomes to maintain that framework. To resolve the tension we have to change either what we do or what we believe.[20]

The four responses surveyed in the previous section represent attempts to change the church, or the believer's thinking and acting, in order to respond adequately to the challenges of change. Thus, we attempt to make our way as individuals by devising our own religious program, aided variously by books, preachers, gurus, and other seekers; or we seek guidance to strengthen our capacity to decide what to do within the various situations of our lives; or we scale up the church, hoping to increase its corporate influence; or we seek to concentrate and draw as much of life as we can into the church segment. Many of us have pursued more than one of these approaches, either in succession or in combination. But in the end it has become apparent to most of us, Strivers, Challengers, and Calculators alike, that these responses do not produce a framework that includes God and the church integrated with all, or nearly all, our daily living. And our irretrievable loss of the country (to recall Peter Schrag's image) includes the loss of the social base on which to *re*construct such a framework as well.

Consider, for example, the implications of that loss for one of the basic tenets of the Christian faith: what theologians call Providence. According to this doctrine, God is envisioned as effectively present in all of life. The external pattern of a traditional community, with its interconnectedness and visible presence of the church to all of life, supports a framework that testifies to the Providence of God. Indeed, in such a world, as we have seen, the presence of God seems inescapable.

By contrast, the pattern of our now-urbanized society, with its unconnected segments, argues against the traditional view of Providence, largely because another connection that many of us have long taken for granted has become a problem. Most of us (perhaps unconsciously) have depended on the pervasive presence of the church to demonstrate the pervasive presence of God. But the presence of the church in all of life is *not* obvious to most people anymore. In fact, for many people, it is not apparent at all in some segments. The connection that once helped us has now become a problem. We can no longer see how God can be effective wherever we can no longer perceive the presence of the church. In these portions of our lives the experience of God's *absence* is reinforced each day. Then, perhaps, God is effectively "dead" in these segments?

Increasingly the official theological framework of the church, which, in general, includes a traditional understanding of Providence, represents a world view that fewer and fewer of its members actually experience. Those whose daily living supports such an "official" framework of belief are now a cognitive minority in contemporary society. This minority includes people who, for various reasons, can protect themselves against social change and others who, like the "locals" described earlier in this chapter, are least affected by the social change that accompanies urbanization. The fact that such people are most likely to be involved in local churches now becomes even more understandable. Their framework of belief tends to coincide with the church's "official" framework of belief because that "official" framework is more often supported by their daily experience. Like theologians and clergy who articulate the official church position, locals and other similarly protected people spend most of their time in a social environment where the church's influence is apparent.

The dilemma the rest of us experience is well described in an essay by Louis Dupres. After outlining the lack of objective bases for belief in modern society, Dupres goes on to say: "Religious men and women will continue to attribute a 'sacred' quality to persons, objects, and events closely connected with their relation to the transcendent. But they will do so because they *hold* them to be sacred, not because they *perceive* them as sacred."[21] The reality of God is no longer generally apparent; it is individually determined. Each of us decides what to believe.

Few of us, however, can stand alone in our faith. To maintain faith, most of us require what Peter Berger calls a "plausibility structure"—a network of relationships and experiences that repeatedly reinforces and supports the plausibility of what we believe.

> Worlds [Berger uses this word roughly in the same way that I use "frameworks"] are socially constructed and socially maintained. Their continuing reality, both objective . . . and subjective . . . , depends upon *specific* social processes, namely those processes that ongoingly reconstruct the (objective and subjective) reality of the worlds in question. . . . Thus each world requires a social "base" for its continuing existence, as a world that is real to actual human beings. This "base" may be called its plausibility structure."[22]

The interconnected reality of God and church with all of life in a traditional community or neighborhood provides such a plausibility structure. The overarching presence of the church supports the general perception that God is effectively present in all of life.

What happens when the plausibility structure that supports a framework breaks down, as ours has in the recent disconnections of space and time? How do we continue to believe when the evidence we have trusted is no longer apparent? The church is no longer able to demonstrate the reality of God's presence in all of life *convincingly.* Yet the church continues to teach that God is effectively present to all of life. In such a situation we are likely to conclude that what the church teaches about God is, at least to some extent, not true.[23] How much and where we are not sure.

Our framework is undermined. Under the pressure of a challenge like Susan faced at work, when, even after we seek guidance from the church, we are still not clear about what we should do, or how God will help us, the loss seems devastating indeed. There is no firm plausibility structure to return to anymore to discover for sure what we can and should do "out there." To build on Peter Schrag's image, we have lost not only the country, but the country church as well. In the same way that we can no longer go back to Main Street to discover visible evidence of how to live, we can no longer go back to the church on the corner to discover what we can believe. Both are integrated into a way of life that has been undermined by change. And we have not been able to either stop the world or get off.

More and more, we are like those suburban church members among whom I ministered thirty years ago. Many of us sing the same hymns we have always sung, but only some of us still believe that the world they describe actually exists. Yet, not knowing what else to do or how to describe God's role clearly in many segments of our lives, we sing on nostalgically—and hopefully. But not all of us do. Some of us have forgotten the old songs; others among us see no reason to learn the old songs—or to try to believe through the old framework.

CHAPTER FIVE

Believing Through Our Own Times

No one asked me to read the works of William James during my years as a seminary student. In fact, I had practiced ministry for nearly a decade before my narrow theological perspective was challenged by James' insights concerning religious experience. That troubling might have come from any one of a number of other thinkers—as I was to discover later. But none of them were then on the theological student's reading list.

Believing from the Believer's Perspective

In those days most seminaries encouraged students to focus exclusively on classic, theological concerns. With the exception of courses in pastoral skills—Christian education and preaching—a "theological" seminary was viewed as a place to pursue "theological" studies. My own introduction at seminary to current and past biblical and systematic theology was excellent. I learned well what Reformed Christians are supposed to believe. Fortunately, nearly all of what was taught set well with me, and still does, because the content of biblical theology largely coincides with my own religious experience.

During those years in seminary the tasks of ministry were also defined for me largely in "evangelical" terms. As a minister I was to be clear about correct belief and show others how to find it. As a pastor I was to "preach the word" and *"instruct"* others in the faith.

When I became an ordained minister I discovered that most church members expected me to be what the seminary taught me to be. I instructed and people listened. As a matter of fact, during the early years of my ministry only a few unusually courageous lay persons challenged me face to face about *anything* I said. Even in Sunday school classes composed of well-educated adults it was difficult to facilitate *any* discussion. Most people's attitude seemed to imply "You know what is right, Pastor; we trust you to tell us what we should believe." The few people who asked more than an occasional question in a class were viewed by the rest of the class as troublesome; others wanted them to be quiet so I could get on with "the lesson."

Those lay persons whose believing earned the admiration of other church members were popularly described as "pillars of faith." Typically, they were people who had experienced some significant adversity but who still held firmly to their faith. They were people who not only accepted "the faith," but also never never complained about what God or life brought to them. Other church members seldom asked the "pillars" how or why they kept on believing in spite of the disasters that had come to them; they just admired them. (Looking back, I suspect that the other church members did not want to question the "pillars," testimony to the fundamental reliability of the church's teachings because no one wanted to challenge the framework on which everyone depended.)

Moving from no faith to faith usually meant accepting what "Christians believe" or "what the church teaches." More conservative denominations usually insisted on assent to a few specific statements (e.g., to "accept Jesus Christ as your personal Lord and Savior"). But the focus was clearly theological. To believe meant to accept well-defined *beliefs,* to assent to proper theological statements about what God is like, what God intends, and what God wants humans to be and do. And to trust that the system of belief the church represents is sound whenever and however one might be puzzled personally.

The unchurched and the unbelievers were thought of as one in the same. The more conservative church members described them as "the lost" (especially when trying to raise money for missions). Those who were more moderate envisioned them less ultimately: as adherents to "primitive" religions or as lacking the "fullness of faith" that Christians possessed. Closest of all were the Jews, who were seen benevolently as almost enlightened, our kin in the Judeo-Christian tradition.

However generous and tolerant we might feel about them, all unchurched persons were seen, at least to some degree, as erroneous believers. The pervading attitude of most of us in those years is crystallized in the reported conversation between an unusually perceptive Third World Christian and a not-so-perceptive First World theologian. On hearing the theologian offer a description of the "errors" of Buddhists' beliefs, the Third World Christian asks him whether he has ever talked *directly* with Buddhists about their beliefs.

"No," the theologian responds.

"Why not?" the Christian continues.

"Because Buddhists are wrong!"

Against such a background it is little wonder that I was startled as I read through William James during those quiet winter mornings. Quite apart from what he said specifically, the overall approach James suggests challenged me to consider believing from a new and contrasting perspective: the *believer's.* I was soon launched on a twenty-year journey of doing just that.

James suggests precisely the perspective on believing against which I

had been cautioned: listening to what people define as their own religious experiences *and taking them seriously.* Implicitly I had been taught *not* to listen seriously to people's descriptions of their own religious experiences and perspectives, except to be able to point out ("gently, but firmly") where they were correct and where they were in error. From that strictly theological perspective, the believer's own religious experience is of little account. When the "teachings of the church" show clearly what we are supposed to believe, then unique or puzzling or contradictory religious experiences and perspectives that may intrude themselves are either fantasy or evidence of immaturity or problems or errors or perhaps even sinful. The challenge to the believer is not to interpret these experiences, but to correct them, or get over them.

Church members among whom I ministered generally conformed to what was expected of them. Hardly anyone in the churches I served talked about or even admitted to having personal religious experiences. As a pastor I was supposed to have close experiences with God (within a classic, Christian mode, of course). Some people thought that it was even *necessary* for me to have my own religious experiences in order to be a minister. But few wanted such experiences for themselves, or thought they were even appropriate for "ordinary" Christians. Many of them believed that firsthand religious experiences are too risky for lay persons, probably because they lack the theological training necessary to determine whether such experiences are authentic or good.

Personal religious experiences also seemed unnecessary to most people then. In a traditional, integrated community the church is visibly in touch with all of life. There most people assume the church can define what everybody ought to believe and do. When questions arise the theologically educated pastor, who also is in touch with all aspects of life, can interpret and apply the beliefs of the church to whatever doubtful situations become apparent. The role of lay persons is to be faithful to the church and seek its guidance. In such a situation doing our own believing is not only risky, but also unnecessary.

Once social change disintegrates the world in which we live, it also undermines much of the effectiveness of the traditional church and pastor in our lives. We can no longer depend on the adequacy of church and pastor. In most of life we are on our own, far away from the presence of church and pastor. The integrated church world is gone. Life presents us with situations that are unprecedented. Then we can't "find" our way because there is no established way to find. We have to "make" our way, and that takes considerably more effort and innovation. Of believing as well as living.

Even different Christians in the same congregation now often discover that they approach believing from different perspectives and with different assumptions. For example, some of the young people who sought my guidance as a pastor during the difficult years of the war in Vietnam wondered what God wanted them to do. So did their parents. Generally, they and their parents came to different conclusions. And generally, I was unable to help the young people and their parents "see things the same."

It was frustrating indeed. The young people and their parents were living in the same church and nation but seeing them quite differently. They still do. The differences in perspective and approach to believing were not caused (as the parents seemed to think) by the young people's lack of experience and maturity. The same young people are maturer now, some of the "rougher edges" have worn off, and they may be less vocal, but they still see church and nation differently from their parents.

As shown in chapter 3, these young people and their parents belong to different cohorts and, for this reason, relate to the world through different frameworks. Challengers' experience during the war in Vietnam was an obvious example of their overall experience of the world as largely uncharted terrain, through which they need to make their way. Their Striver parents' lack of sympathetic understanding is based, to some extent, in a lack of awareness (or acceptance) of the extent of social change, and perhaps in a fear of social change. Strivers' approach is akin to that hunger to hang on to "rural" roots, the belief that the real world is a stable world in which everything remains constant and clear, including the fact that when called on by their country, citizens should always fight for their country. As I listened to them I could hear in my memory the words of the scout oath I had learned as a twelve-year-old: "On my honor I will do my best to do my duty to God and my country." More often than not, in those years Striver parents wanted me, as a pastor representing the church, to attest to the continuing existence of that stable world, especially to their Challenger children, whose behavior in response to the war (and a variety of other social crises) was challenging the conventions on which their way of life depended.

For me the dilemma came into sharp focus when I listened sympathetically to *both* points of view. I listened to Strivers explain why they believed God wanted them to fight for their country in World War II and why the young people should do the same in this war. I listened to Challengers explain why they believed God wanted them to protest against the war in Vietnam. And they *both* convinced me! They were each being faithful *within their own times.*

My reading and reflecting and experiences since my seminary days had challenged my narrow, seminary-shaped theological perspective. As a result I listened to what each person believed he or she should do as a Christian *through that person's life experience*. I moved from each person's living to each person's believing. And I saw clearly for the first time how their different approaches to believing are shaped necessarily and legitimately by their unique experiences. I can diagram the insight:

Person ⟶ God

Note that I did not draw:

Person ⟵ God

The first diagram portrays the relationship of a person with God *from the person's perspective*. The second diagram shows the relationship of a person

with God *from God's viewpoint*. I now believe that appropriate theology considers *both* perspectives.

We can consider the relationship from either perspective. When we look at the relationship from one perspective we gain different insights than we do when we consider it from the other.

From the second perspective, Person ←——— God, we can explore such questions as "What is God like?" and "What should people believe?" From the first perspective, Person ———→ God, we can explore such questions as "What does Person A believe God is like?" and "Why does he or she believe that?"

In this book I have focused on believing from the first perspective. The second, which was the nearly exclusive concern of my theological education and of most of the church members among whom I began my work as a pastor, is not more or less important; it is simply different. From the second perspective what Person A (or any other person) currently believes is of only secondary concern. But from the first perspective what Person A currently believes is of central concern. Right or wrong, from the second perspective, that is Person A's current framework. To make a connection with Person A (I shall amplify what I mean by this phrase in chapter 6), those of us who are concerned to share the Christian faith need to consider both perspectives.

We can also amplify either diagram to portray a shared framework:

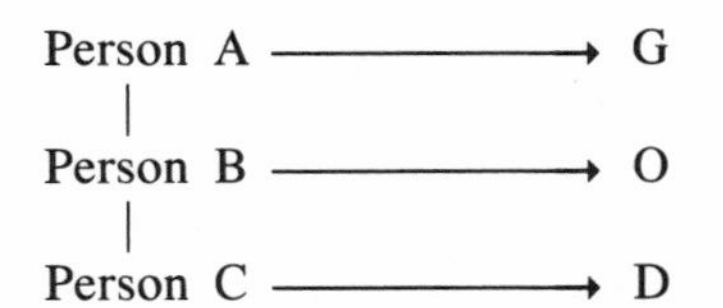

In the rest of this chapter I shall explore how our shared frameworks can shape our approach to believing. In the next chapter I shall embrace both perspectives and suggest ways in which understanding Christians can share their faith with those who are not Christian.

The parents and young people whom I have been using as examples were both trying to discover a faithful, Christian response to a serious question. Unfortunately for both, a lack of respect for the validity of the other's shared framework kept them apart. They were unable to be of much help to each other.

No one can describe adequately or fairly how any person in particular should respond to "what a Christian should do" unless one appreciates where in space and time that person lives, or, to use some perceptive slang, is "coming from." The young people and their parents weren't talking about war in general (although, unfortunately, both groups often insisted they were); each group was describing how they believed they should respond to a particular war at a particular place and time *on the basis of their different prime-time life experience*. But because each group insisted on the legitimacy of their own framework alone, the beliefs of the other group seemed unethical to them and not at all what God would want. Whenever we are unwilling to accept the frameworks of others as legitimate, we have difficulty helping them to believe and live responsibly. We tend to be helpful only to those who see things the way we do.

How Life Experiences Shape Believing

Each of us lives into believing uniquely, but not haphazardly. There are coherent patterns to our believing that stem from our basic life experiences. At critical times during our development those whose judgment we trust help us define not only how we will approach living, but also how we will approach believing. The fundamental roles in this process are played, initially, by those close to us when we are children and, later, by those who compose our cohort. What we believe during our adult life reflects what we retain from our childhood, revised and refined primarily by insights we share with our compatriots in time, who usually seem to us to see the world as it really is. And probably God as well.

In our present society, even among Christians, there is no single, accepted, overall approach to believing, just as there is no single, accepted, overall approach to living. Christians historically approached living and believing within a variety of established traditions. But in addition to those classic differences, Christians today approach believing within the same prime-time frameworks as they approach life as a whole. For more than a decade now I have watched and listened to and talked with Strivers, Challengers, and Calculators who are or have been associated with churches in order to discover how their unique prime-time socializations are reflected in their approaches to believing as well as their approaches to living. Then I have asked, on the basis of what they have lived through and believe, how do those in each cohort tend to approach the church, and how might the church approach them? The rest of this chapter is concerned with these questions.

First, I shall share some life stories that combine insights I have gained from many individuals. I have slightly altered some details in each person's story to protect the identity of those who have openly shared with me. But the stories they "relate" are based on the experiences, statements, and beliefs of real people. Each narrator reflects the unique approach that members of her or his cohort take to living and believing and the church.

STRIVERS: Stewart and Stella

Every summer Stella and I go back to feel our roots again on the farm in New Hampshire where I was raised. Mom is gone now, but Dad, even though he's eighty-five, insists on putting in a garden every spring and feeding the chickens every day and tending the stoves all winter. My sister, Anne, still keeps the house and puts up their food for the winter; she never married. Every year she says Dad won't make it through another one, but he always does.

Our Model A truck still sits beside the barn, rusting. It quit some time after I left home. Every time I look at it I can recall those winter days during the Depression when my brother, Pete, and Dad and I would get up at four A.M. to do the barn chores, fill the radiator with water (we couldn't afford alcohol), start the truck, and head for a woodlot. On a good day Pete and I, working opposite ends of a saw, could fell and cut up eight cords of pulpwood. Dad would haul it to the mill—two cords at a time. They paid him two dollars a cord. When the sun dropped we'd go back home, drain the radiator, do the barn chores, have our supper, and go to bed—and do it all over the next day. Except Sundays. And when I had to go to school. I started working my end of the two-man saw in 1937, when I was twelve.

I'd be on that farm yet, except for the War. Toward the end of 1943 I enlisted in the Army. As a farm worker I could have stayed out, but we decided Pete and Dad could make the farm go. So I did my duty.

I've never talked much to Stella about what it was like. Except during those months in the late forties, when I couldn't get by my depression. Two days especially kept coming back into my head. The first was the day we made the beach in France. When we landed there were 171 in my company. An hour later there were thirty-five. Guys were blown apart all around me. Then a couple of days later I killed a boy. "Somebody get the sniper!" the sergeant yelled. I did. When I turned him over he was crying. Looked to be only thirteen or fourteen years old. He bled to death while I was holding him. I can see him look at me yet. I couldn't even tell him I was sorry.

"You did what you had to," the guy told me at the VA hospital. But I couldn't move on. If I hadn't believed all through those months that I was fighting for Stella and my dad and the farm, I'd have laid down in the mud and gone crazy.

In 1946 I married Stella. We would have done it sooner but Stella's mom died the summer before I enlisted. She couldn't leave home until her sister was old enough to take charge of the farmhouse. In 1946 I was discharged and her sister grew up, so we got married.

The GI Bill sent me to college. Stella and I went. We were lucky; we got into the veterans' housing and she got a job as a secretary.

When I graduated in 1950 I started the next week with National Electric. We moved to St. Louis, joined a Presbyterian church, and started a family. There were some pretty tough times during those first ten years. For half of them I was a traveling auditor, sometimes away for two or three weeks. But Stella's a good sport; she's always kept things together at home. We each did our jobs. I've worked hard, but National's been good to us—even after my heart attacks.

In 1975 the church gave me a certificate of appreciation: for twenty-five years of continuous service. They should have given Stella one too. Between us we've done all the jobs. The pastor says he's grateful we're still there every Sunday, now that we live twenty miles away, out in the country.

But I promised God I'd make it up to him, if he got me through the War. Besides, the church needs us.

Sometimes it wasn't easy to stay with the church. The sixties were the toughest; things kind of got mixed up. We had a couple of ministers who kept telling us we needed to get "involved." One started some groups; Stella and I joined one for a while. But we had to quit when I was negotiating with the union during the long strike at National in 1967. That pastor kept telling us to see things more from the workers' viewpoint. He couldn't see reality. If we gave in to the union, our labor costs would go so high that the Japanese would edge us right out of the market. They nearly did anyway.

During the War I saw what happens when people compromise their sense of right and wrong—and that you have to protect yourself and those you love. Once you start giving in, you may not be able to stop.

To be honest, it's been hard for Stella and me to accept some of the stuff our kids have done. Like our son's decision in 1968, when he turned eighteen, to register as a CO and then his dropping out of church and dabbling in strange religions. True, he did finally finish college, and now he's got a job of sorts—taking care of retarded people in some group home. But he still seems to me to be wandering around trying to figure out who he is and what he wants. He's even living with some guy; we're not too keen about that.

But then we weren't crazy about Mary moving in with Kevin either. We've grown to like him, but they've been together two years and they're still not married.

Our only kid left in church is the youngest, Carl, and he's not even in our church. He's joined the new Bible Church down the road from where we live. Now he tells us that what we've done and believed all our lives isn't good enough. Well, I told him we've done what we thought was right. But we have learned not to talk about church with him.

Frankly, the only one of our kids that seems normal to us is our daughter Annie. She married Peter just as soon as they got out of college. They've got two kids now and a nice house outside of Columbus, where he works. We just wish they lived closer.

CHALLENGERS: Charlene and Chuck.

Chuck and I were in school the day it happened. I can remember all of us watching the TV in the lunchroom. We were all crying. I was only seventeen that November day when JFK was shot, but I felt like my world was ending. To be honest, it never really has been the same.

I had just turned fourteen in 1960 when Kennedy was elected President. That summer Mom and Dad bought the big house. I had my own bedroom and my own phone—even my own TV. I was captivated by the Democratic convention. All my friends were. We thought JFK offered the possibility of a new beginning—if he could win. Dad said he wouldn't; people wouldn't elect a Catholic. But he did! And then he was shot. And we all cried all day.

The next time I cried that much was the day Dad threw my brother, Chuck, out of the house. Only that time I was angry. It was the day Chuck told Dad he had registered as a CO. At least Chuck had the guts to put his beliefs on the line.

But they got him anyway. He went to Vietnam as a noncombatant troop-carrier driver. While he was over there he wrote to me twice a week. Sometimes the letters came in bunches. The more I read, the angrier I got—and there was a lot he couldn't tell me until he got back. Five times that thing he drove was hit or blown out from under him. Day after day he'd haul men out simply to watch them get shot up for no reason and to get nowhere. The whole time he was over there nothing changed, except more of them kept getting killed and maimed.

That was the same year I convinced them to show the film at the church service. We'd gotten a new associate pastor the previous summer. He was a *real* minister—had the guts to confront people with what was really going on. He used the film as his sermon that Sunday. The film is called *The Bombs*. In the first part it shows good-looking American flyers loading their bombs and then flying their airplanes off into the beautiful blue sky. The second part shows what happens to the people down below when the bombs hit.

There was a former bomber pilot from World War II there that day; he broke down in the middle and had to leave. People were really angry; they said we shouldn't have done that sort of thing in church. I said the church teaches "Thou shalt not kill" and that includes bombing people—even North Vietnamese. It was eighteen years before I went into a church again.

When Chuck got out of the service he didn't go back to church either. For that matter, he couldn't seem to fit himself into anything. He couldn't forget what he saw over there, and everybody he tried to talk to about it seemed to pretend it had never happened. So he started reading a lot and spending most of his time by himself. For a while he was into drugs. Then he joined a community practicing Zen; I think that helped him get it together more than anything else he tried.

Still I don't think he's ever really gotten by Vietnam. "Why did I go?" he wondered out loud one day when we were talking about it. "Why was I one of the stupid suckers who got stuck with the dirty work? I can't figure out whether I'm a fool or a bastard."

The spring after I left the church Phil and I moved into an attic apartment near the university. For three years we marched and drank wine and got stoned—and sometimes we went to classes. Then we had a child, got married, and got divorced. For the next few years Molly and I had to make it on our own; it wasn't easy earning my own living and raising a child. I tried therapy and joined a women's support group.

Then Bill came along and, to be honest, I was relieved. Even at thirty-four you sense your options are starting to shrink. We've been together long enough to be clear about what we can expect from each other, what to try to share and what to leave alone.

I went back to church several weeks ago—by myself. I don't know why; I just wanted to. Sure enough, the second time I went, after the service the minister came to call. He wasn't in the apartment more than ten minutes before he asked me what my "husband" does and whether he was home. I asked him whether he had come to see me or to see my "husband." Both," he replied. "Well," I said, "in the first place he's not my husband, and in the second place I'm the one that's into church right now; he's into racquetball."

CALCULATORS: Carolyn and Calvin

It didn't seem fair! The week I got my permit you couldn't buy any gas! And then my mother lecturing me, "Carolyn, you're lucky it's not like it was in the War when *everything* was rationed." She sounded like President Carter, when he made that speech telling everybody we should deal with energy shortages by sacrificing like they did during World War II. Who remembers that?

I suppose I should have known what to expect. I've spent most of my life competing. In the sixth grade we were the first kids to go to the new middle school, and we had to eat in shifts because the cafeteria wasn't big enough. My father told me to stop complaining; he could hardly pay the school tax as it was, let alone pay more to build yet another school building.

My folks always seemed to make a lot of money and always complained that it wasn't enough. They complained about a lot of things. Every summer, when we went up to the lake, Dad complained about the trash in the lake and talked about how good the fishing used to be, before there were so many people coming to the lake. I remember once I told him how we had learned in school that acid rain caused by the big industries was the problem. He really got mad! He went on and on about how the damn environmentalists and their regulations were going to put his company out of business.

I was thirteen when my older sister got busted for possession, and fifteen when Mom and Dad split for good. They thought I would be surprised, but I'd known what they were up to for a long time; I wasn't blind. Calvin (he's my younger brother) and I commuted between them for the next few years, until we grew up and got out. It was painful but good for me. I made two decisions before I graduated from high school: if I get married, I'm not going to do it until I know exactly what I want; and I'm not going to take any chances about being able to stand on my own.

I've stuck to both. I worked hard enough in high school to get a full scholarship to go to college. After college I went right on to law school.

When I graduated I took a job with the firm whose offer combined the most security with the most opportunity. In the first year I learned all the technical stuff—and I learned how to impress. It took a lot of late nights, but it was worth it. While my older sister is whining about how tough it is to make it in a man's world, I do it. I earned sixty thousand dollars last year and this year I'll make even more.

Every so often Mom asks me when I will get married. "Some day," I always tell her. It's true my friend Carl and I spend lots of time together, but we are both committed to our careers right now. You can't do everything, especially not all at once; you have to know what your priorities are.

Calvin sure knows his. He decided not to go on to school, said he'd rather work. Besides, he says he's not impressed with how people think who have been to college. After one term he dropped out and began working for a mason. Calvin really hustles; in record time he did his appenticeship, got his own union card, and bought his own truck.

The summer he married Carrie he landed a contract to do all the foundation work for one of the most active contractors in the area where he lives. Sometimes Carrie complains that she doesn't see much of Calvin. Then he reminds her that she doesn't have to go out to work like I do and like Mom did after she and Dad split.

Of course, Calvin doesn't ever work on Sunday. "Sunday is the Lord's day," he points out to me, when I tell him I've spent the weekend skiing or have to catch a plane on Sunday to be ready to work with a client somewhere early on Monday. "The Lord has never managed to catch up with me!" I once snickered. "He will," Calvin said. And he didn't smile.

How Cohorts Approach Living

Members of the three cohorts do exhibit some fundamentally different approaches to living and believing and the church. To point up their distinguishing characteristics, I have listed some of their contrasting approaches to living in Table 5:1 and some of their contrasting approaches to believing and the church in Table 5:2 (page 84).

Table 5:1 How Cohorts Approach Living

Strivers	*Challengers*	*Calculators*
Stability is normal	Change is normal	Erosion is normal
Defend our way of life	Alter and expand our way of life	Choose and conserve what matters most
Alternatives	Options	Consequences

Oughts; begin with obligations	Wants; begin with interests	Possibilities; begin with constraints

We can see how Strivers, Challengers, and Calculators act out their distinctive approaches to living by analyzing the life histories we have just traced. To make it easy to recall who belongs to which cohort, I gave each person a name that begins with the same first two letters as his or her cohort name: *St*ewart and *St*ella are *St*rivers; *Ch*arlene and *Ch*uck are *Ch*allengers; *Ca*rolyn, *Ca*lvin and *Ca*rrie are *Ca*lculators.

We will consider each set of comparisons in turn.

Stability is normal | **Change is normal** | **Erosion is normal**

For Strivers, like Stewart and Stella, the stable world is normal. Their approach to living depends on the world continuing as it has been in the past. Whatever change they may experience, they feel that someday, somehow things will quiet down and "get back to normal." Thus, change for Strivers usually means development, not transition. Stewart comes back from the war and picks up where he left off. Even today he can go home to the farm and see that things are still as they were. When he faces the trauma of his war experience he falls back to find a steady social context that provides him with the support and reassurance he needs. The stress and sacrifices he has had to endure make sense. His stable world affirms and supports him.

Not so Chuck's. The Challenger framework through which Chuck experiences life does not prescribe clear roles he should play. He has to define the role he will play in the war. He returns from his service to reenter an ambiguous society that sometimes affirms and sometimes damns him for what he has done. The church in his experience does not offer a comprehensive, overarching framework to help him orient himself in the years that follow his discharge from the service. Chuck has to make his own way, largely on his own, without the aid of institutions and tradition. Fluidity, not stability, is the normal state of affairs in his life.

As it is for his sister. When her church will not change to oppose what seems to her to be an unjust war, Charlene moves out of it. Her life from then on is more like a series of shifting roles than an intentional pattern: college, marriage, divorce, single parent, career. If things within and around her were to settle down, that would not be normal. She, like most Challengers, expects life to be filled with constant change. In fact, when given the opportunity to move into a stable environment like so many Strivers seek, most Challengers do not; they feel such a life would be too dull and confining.

Carolyn, as a Calculator, functions somewhat the same as Charlene and Chuck, but with much less trauma. She is not surprised by society's instability and lack of consensus. She expects continuing social change; from childhood she and her peers have faced difficult decisions. But unlike

Challengers, who during their early years were enchanted by what they envisioned as ever-expanding options, Carolyn, like nearly all Calculators, has had to choose in a world of shrinking options. As a result, she and Calvin approach living soberly and prudently; they make their choices with lowered vision in what appears to them to be a world of limited resources and opportunities.

Defend our way of life	**Alter and expand our way of life**	**Choose and conserve what matters most**

When "our way of life" is threatened, as it was during the World War II years, Stewart and Stella rise quickly and firmly to defend it. They see the basic institutions of life—the family, nation, and church—as inherently good, to be protected, not changed.

By Chuck and Charlene's era the same institutions are under severe criticism, especially from their peers. They challenge the nation's involvement in the war in Vietnam and the adequacy of the government's concern for minorities and women. They question the church's expected role of supporting our side in the war and want it to play an untypical, "disordering" role in the social revolution. Among those who compose their cohort, the traditional family has had to make room for other options: intentionally childless marriages, single parents, single persons who live together, and those who simply perfer to stay single. Beginning in affluence, with a heady sense of their own limitless potential, Challengers presume they will be able to correct most ills while indulging their own wants. For a while.

Not so the Calculators. Their basic attitudes are much less likely to be colored by such illusions, either about their individual potential or the potential of humankind as a whole. In fact many, if not most, Challengers have *never* experienced a time when humanity as a whole, even the earth itself, has not been threatened by destruction. In their framework every tomorrow might become "The Day After" the nuclear holocaust, to recall the title of a deeply moving 1983 television program. "The most cautious of mediums," *Newsweek* predicted, ". . . will reach out and detonate a thermonuclear apocalypse in our communal psyche." Suddenly, into the midst of the ordinary activities of ordinary people "come four minutes of the most horrifying searing footage ever to pass a network censor: building implosions, group immolations, a carnage of mass vaporizations. And when it all settles, the starkest nightmare ever broadcast has only just begun."[1]

In a follow-up article, "When Kids Think the Unthinkable," Marcia Yudkin looks back through research over the past decade to describe the pall cast over children's and teenagers' growing-up years by the nuclear threat. She writes of fifth graders who have "nightmares about everyone except them being blown up by bombs, leaving them alone and helpless."[2] Yudkin cites Jerald Bachman's longitudinal study of the concerns of high school graduating seniors. Between 1975 and 1982 the percentage of those who worried about nuclear war rose from 7.2 percent to 31.2 percent. In 1982 more than a third of all seniors agreed with the statement "Nuclear or biological annihilation will probably be the fate of all mankind within my lifetime."[3]

Against such a backdrop, those in Calvin and Carolyn's cohort are much more prudent and careful than the Challengers who precede them. Always seeking to calculate the consequences of their decisions, they choose and intently pursue what they believe to be the best of the possibilities available to them. Calculators have an overall feeling that life itself is contingent on one's daily choices.

Alternatives Options Consequences

Stewart and Stella, like most Strivers, see life as composed of alternatives to be faced: right or wrong, a good way to live or a bad way, a good side to be on (ours) or a bad side (the enemy's). Moral behavior consists of honoring absolutes: if you work hard enough, you will succeed; fight for your country when called on to do so; sex belongs in marriage, not before it, and, of course, is never right between persons of the same sex.

As Challengers, Charlene and her friends seldom see their choices confined to rigid alternatives. They are much more likely to think expansively, in terms of options. Their attitudes toward relationships between the sexes, for example, are much less rigid and more experimental. Sex is experienced more like a want, more in terms of pleasure or fun than in terms of morality. A wide range of books offering permission and suggestions for ways to have sexual fun is available.

The war in Vietnam does not seem like a war fought to defend our civilization. Nor does everyone see an obviously good side and bad side to be on in this war, as the film Charlene convinces the associate minister to show during the worship service seeks to demonstrate. There are various legitimate and revealing perspectives from which to see ourselves and our adversaries.

Calvin also faces an ambiguous world, but as a Calculator, he is prepared to make and be confined by his choices. Like the Challengers, he thinks in terms of options rather than alternatives. But unlike the Challengers, Calvin believes the course of his entire life tomorrow will be limited by his choices today. He sees shrinking, not expanding, possibilities and sets out early to protect the options he wants to guarantee for himself. And as Carrie, his wife, understands clearly, anyone who wants to keep pace with him will have to fall into line.

Calculators, on the whole, are much more decisive than Challengers, perhaps because so many of them were forced to grow up quickly, and have seen or experienced the adverse consequences of others' choices. Or of their own. In *Children Without Childhood* Marie Winn describes Challengers as children growing up with the consequences of permissiveness, struggling to cope with early exposures to sex and drugs—and most of all with life after their parents' divorces.[4] Lee Goldberg, a child during this era, writes in the

March 1983 *Newsweek on Campus* of his own forced early growing up. (He was a junior at the University of California at Los Angeles when he wrote the article.)

> In divorce, parents seem to become teen-agers, and the kids become the adults. . . . As our parents pursued careers and re-entered the dating scene, we children coped by forming our own little mini-families, with the older kids parenting for the younger siblings. It was common for single mothers to joke about how their eldest son played doting father, checking out her dates and offering sage advice. . . . Divorce didn't just split up our parents. It stole our childhood.[5]

Many Calculators cannot remember a time when they didn't have to be responsible.

Oughts; begin with obligations	**Wants; begin with interests**	**Possibilities; begin with constraints**

For Strivers, the core of life is duty. Satisfaction is a reward deserved only by those who fulfill their obligations well to nation, church, family, and work. Play is what one does after all obligations are met—if there is time.

Challengers, born of affluence, are more likely to honor their wants, to work only as necessary, and even then to believe that work itself should be a rewarding experience. In times of questioning (e.g., what to do about an unhappy marriage or work situation) they are at least as likely to ask themselves what they want to do as they are to think about what they ought to do. Constitutionally, Challengers feel they *should* be able to live according to their wants.[6] They even seek therapy when they are unable to want without feeling guilty.

Calculators choose among options and commit themselves to what each of them sees as possible and desirable for him or her personally. For example, Carrie and Carolyn make different choices between marriage and career. Calvin, like Stewart and Stella's Calculator son Carl, chooses beliefs and a church that meet his own needs and criteria. Although Calvin views his sister's way of life as eternally disastrous, he doesn't challenge her right to choose it. What all Calculators have in common in their shared framework is the belief that they can and must choose, and that they won't be able to have and do everything. Living, for them, is the art of the possible.

How Cohorts Approach Believing and the Church

Strivers, Challengers, and Calculators approach believing and the church within patterns that are consistent with their distinctive approaches to living. Their approaches to believing and the church are outlined in Table 5:2.

Table 5:2 How Cohorts Approach Believing and the Church

Strivers	*Challengers*	*Calculators*
God is taken for granted and seen as essential	God is defined personally and is optional	God is defined and seen as essential by believers only
Church is central, a stabilizing force	Church is marginal, a social advocate	Churches play a variety of roles
Morality predominates	Ethics predominates	Piety predominates
Expect to support church and be cared for; to be loyal to church; to belong	Expect church to support my needs and causes; to find meaning from church; to act	Believers expect church to nurture and support them; to gain resources from church; to survive

God is one of life's givens for Strivers, the core of the American way of life. We are a nation under God. Strivers are good "scouts" who do their duty to God and country.

Many Strivers with whom I have talked recall a public school day that opened with the teacher or a student reading some verses from the Bible, the class joining in the Lord's Prayer and then the Pledge of Allegiance to the American flag. Many regret the loss of this tradition that "teaches children to believe in God."

People who don't believe in God do not seem normal to Strivers. They appear as curiosities, people who, for some reason, do not believe "what we all know is true." To some Strivers, unbelievers appear unpatriotic or dangerous because their lack of believing undermines the American way.

Doctrinal differences seldom trouble Strivers personally. For example, when I have asked them (following Martin Marty's suggestion) whether they favor Southern Baptist prayer or Jewish prayer or Black Muslim prayer if prayer should be restored as the norm in public schools, my question doesn't make sense to them. Most Strivers assume that because "we all believe in the same God," our praying will be harmonious.

No such harmony and stability mark the religious experience of the Challengers. Challengers were taught to challenge whatever does not seem right to them. In their view, a person's faith in God is demonstrated not by loyalty to the church, but by ethical action. When church members do not appear to act out what they say they believe, Challengers confront them. Charlene, for example, confronts members of her congregation with what she believes is their lack of support for the biblical prohibition against killing. But when she encourages the showing of the film *The Bombs,* she discovers, to her eventual disillusionment, that members of her Striver-dominated congregation follow a national theology. They believe those in the service of their country are not bound by the sixth commandment in a time of war; they do not see their acts of killing in defense of our country as violations of the sixth commandment. She is appalled by what she sees as theological inconsistency and angered at the unwillingness of members of her congregation even to discuss whether the war in Vietnam is morally justifiable. In protest, she leaves the church for nearly twenty years.

Charlene's brother, Chuck, struggles to find the personal resources he needs to cope with his war experience. Probably discouraged by his sister's and others' disappointing experience with the church, he doesn't even try to search for those resources within the church. After a long search he finally seeks help from a Zen master. His picture of God and way of believing are clearly of his own making, drawn from a variety of sources. The variety of belief among Challengers, particularly their attraction to Eastern religious practices, is baffling to Strivers, who do not share Challengers' sense of disillusionment and frustration with institutional religion.

Calculators' approach to believing is usually not so marked by turmoil and frustration as is the Challengers'. But as a group Calculators do reflect more variety than do Strivers. Calculators, like the Challengers who precede them, take the segmented, pluralistic nature of society for granted (although not always happily). Likewise, they see believing as an individual option and responsibility.

But if Challengers are spiritual experimenters, then Calculators are spiritual pragmatists, Calculators want a faith that works. Most follow an approach like Carl's and choose congregations that reflect and support their personal beliefs. Their Striver parents, who seldom seem concerned to refine their personal beliefs, wonder, as Stewart and Stella do, why their Calculator children aren't content with "our" church. But, as shall be seen presently, given their much more specifically religious focus, Calculators want more from a church than a sense they belong and to appear respectable because they do. Calculators want a congregation that nurtures their *faith*.

Believing, however, is not an issue for Calculators like Carolyn. She, like many of those who enjoy an affluent "Yuppie" life-style, appears not to feel empty or confused or inadequate or bad because she is not a believer in the traditional sense. In times of difficulty she, and others like her, is more likely to turn to friends or a counselor for support than to a church or pastor for help to find "the will to go on." Her lack of need for God and church is often baffling to Strivers and sometimes troubling to those Calculators who, like her brother, are committed believers. But few Challengers are troubled by her lack of need or concern for religion. She is simply not "into church." She is preoccupied by other interests she finds more appealing or necessary or helpful.

Church is central, a stabilizing force

Church is marginal, a social advocate

Churches play a variety of roles

Morality predominates	Ethics predominates	Piety predominates
Expect to support church and be cared for; to be loyal to church; to belong	**Expect church to support my needs and causes; to find meaning from church; to act**	**Believers expect church to nurture and support them; to gain resources from church; to survive**

In the Strivers' framework the church is central, an essential, stabilizing force in our society. Going to church and Sunday school are good for you.

Most Strivers see respectable, moral behavior and supporting the church as sufficient evidence that one is a good church member. They continue the pattern Alexis de Tocqueville observed more than a century ago during his visit to the United States: "Go into the churches, you will hear morality preached, of dogma not a word."[7] To hold a job, be economically and sexually responsible, have a good family life, and support country and church are good enough.

Not so for Challengers. They see a good church member as someone who fulfills a much more activist role. They heed not simply the moral commandments of scripture, but also the prophetic injunctions to attack injustice. Challengers believe the church is often called to stand over against unjust practices within those same basic institutions that Strivers feel called simply to affirm. In the Challengers' view, churches and nations have to demonstrate that they are faithful through ethical policies and just actions.

In the Challengers' framework the church is located more often at the edge of society, in the role of a critic and change agent, than in the center, as a normative force maintaining the status quo. Many Challengers are deeply disturbed at the social inequities that continue to mark our society, such as lack of equal opportunities and compensation for women and minorities. They want the church to keep reminding its members of issues many Strivers would just as soon forget.

Perhaps Challengers view the church so differently from the way Strivers do because so few of them remember a society in which the church was effectively present to all of life. The unified framework of God-church-school-nation-family disintegrated during Challengers' prime time. They carry a sense of society's disconnectedness in their frameworks, not its unity. For example, many were attending public school when the prayer and Bible reading that had always begun each day ceased. Challengers felt the world come apart.

Moreover, many Challengers, like Charlene and Chuck, remember specific occasions when they feel the church let them down. And only a few congregations have been able to develop the special resources Challengers need to make their way to faith.

The diversity of viewpoints among Calculators about the necessity of the church has already been noted. Those like Carolyn feel no need for the church. Others hunger for the church to gain more influence in society, especially those concerned about what they perceive as dangerous contemporary moral practices (e.g., abortion on demand, sex education in the public schools).

Some Strivers and Calculators have joined forces in an effort to place the church once again at the center of American life. Although these joint efforts show some success, they are not likely to result in a restoration of the church to its former dominant position in American life. The old, cohesive social order is fragmented beyond the possibility of reassembly. There are as many people today like Charlene and Chuck and Carolyn as there are people like Stewart and Calvin and Carrie and Carl. The overall social consensus that provided support for the church as a dominant influence in all dimensions of life is gone. Those who envision a recovery of the old order are more nostalgic than astute.

Of course, not everyone stays completely within lifeways appropriate to the cohort to which he or she belongs. Understandably, some of us stray. Once the lifeways of a cohort are defined, they become socially available options. Some of us who do not belong to a cohort in terms of age may appropriate some of that cohort's lifeways and incorporate them into our own living.

For example, many young people today appear to be reaffirming elements that usually distinguish the Strivers' approach to living, like the traditional family. At the same time, many people whose age would place them among the Strivers have adopted Challenger attitudes toward marriage and, in middle age, are dissolving marriages that they do not find satisfying. Thus, occasionally, some of us are behind or ahead of our own times.

But it is important not to overestimate the implications of these exceptions. As much as we like to think of ourselves as unique, only a few of us stand apart in a style that does not reflect the overall approach of our compatriots in time. Throughout our lives most of us hold consistently to a pattern that reflects our prime time. Even when we do adopt approaches to living and believing that are more typical of another cohort, we act them out within patterns and feelings peculiar to our native lifeway (e.g., Strivers usually struggle much more with guilt when they divorce than Challengers do; Calculators who seek to recover some of the values of the traditional family often live together for a while before they marry).

After more than a decade of careful study I am convinced that the overall framework into which we are acculturated and the modes of perceiving associated with that framework are remarkably persistent. Each of us approaches living and believing and, if we choose to do so, the church through our socially defined framework. The church that appeals to us and nurtures us will probably approach us through that framework as well. Because that is where we start from.

CHAPTER SIX

Nurturing Christian Faith

Up to this point I have made an effort not to let my Christian faith color my description of the perspectives that shape believing today. I have made that effort because I think all of us need to be aware of the variety of frameworks within which people now function. In order to make appropriate suggestions about believing and living to someone, one needs to understand the perspectives through which *that person* approaches believing and living—perspectives that may be quite different from one's own.

The varied frameworks through which people now approach believing and living offer unique challenges to Christians who feel called to share their faith with others. In a subsequent book I plan to describe in detail some approaches that churches can take to meet these challenges. In the final chapter of this present book I suggest how the perspectives that compose each framework are likely to shape the approach those who live within that framework take to Christian faith as well. Sharing Christian faith in a way that is genuinely helpful requires unusual sensitivity today, not only to God, but to the particular person or persons with whom we seek to share.

Mature Believers Who Are Not Christian

Some years ago I talked with a pastor from New Zealand about the differences between theological education there and in the United States. He saw much to praise about our system but was critical at one point in particular:

> Many of your seminaries, especially the denominational ones, are quite isolated. While they are learning how to be ministers, your students tend to interact only with other theological students and other Christians. As a result most of them are comfortable talking about their faith only with others who are

already convinced Christians. That's not the real world—even in your country.

He is right on both counts: the real world (likely even in the United States) is composed mostly of people who are not Christians, and it is not easy to share our faith with them. Many times I have been frustrated in my own attempts to share Christian faith with those who are not Christians.

I recall one especially difficult experience. It began late on a winter day with the tragic news that a close friend's wife had been killed. For the first few hours I sat with the friend while he struggled with his feelings of disbelief. Had it really happened? Wouldn't she soon come home like she always had?

But she didn't. As the days plodded on he slowly came to terms with the fact that she was really gone. At first he was consumed by wrenching sorrow. But he made no attempt to evade the reality of his feelings, and after a while the hours of all-out pain spaced out more and more. As the raw grief subsided, questions began to surface. "Why was she taken from me?" "How could God, whom you keep saying cares about us, allow such a tragedy to happen?" he asked me.

Again and again we talked, always in the end returning to that last question. After the loss of his wife he was not able to believe that any God who might rule the universe actively cares for people. No response I gave seemed to help. My best theological insights were of no avail. Time after time I shared what I believe about God's sovereignty and caring. I described how I discovered the reality of that caring during my own experiences of grief and tragedy. Although he often told me he was grateful for my persistent attempts to respond to his dilemma, he found no satisfying answer in any of the suggestions I made.

The source of our inability to communicate came to light quite by accident one afternoon, in what appeared at first to be an unrelated conversation. I was sharing with him my childhood image of how God made rain. I described my picture of a giant in the sky sitting before an array of large levers. By pulling the appropriate lever God made rain or snow or sleet, or whatever other weather was the choice for that day.

We had a good laugh over my early picture of God's relationship with the world. But the story stimulated my friend to describe once more why his own understanding of God's relation to the world had been undermined by the experience of his wife's death. What became clear to me for the first time is the mechanical picture he has of that relationship. *Everything* that happens is necessarily caused by a decision and action of the Almighty. In such a world, "if God is in control, then what happens is what God makes happen. Otherwise, how can God be almighty?"

"It makes no sense to pray to God," he went on. "I tried that, and obviously it doesn't work. Perhaps God may have some control, but I have discovered that's no guarantee he will take care of me and those I love."

As my friend continued to talk I was struck again and again by how little his views have in common with Christian theology, as I learned it and believe it. When he finished sharing we talked about the block in our communication, the radical differences in our understandings of God's relationship with the world.

For months, not realizing what we were doing, he and I had been using the same words, like "God" and "caring" and "almighty," but with very different images in our minds. His images are largely mechanical; mine are largely personal. I picture a devoted Creator, who out of grace continues to sustain the created world, despite its now inherent sinfulness. Where I experience God as pained by the tragedy that comes to me (and to others), actively upholding me as I pass through the devastating experiences of my life, he sees God as at fault for the tragedy that has come to him and then as callous and distant when he needs help to survive it. We look at the same world and come to different conclusions. We see the world through different frameworks.

By his own admission my friend is not a Christian and never has been. He was socialized outside the church in a family that is not Christian. He grew up perceiving the world as segmented. The pervasive presence of the church and of the God to whom the church witnesses were never socially apparent to him. He has not internalized in his framework the image of a provident, personal, caring God that many of us who are Christians take for granted.

The fact that I am a minister, trained in Christian theology, does not enable me to help him. During my years as a pastor that identity was often sufficient to encourage others toward Christian faith. Although their own faith might be challenged during times of stress, the fact that I stood with them as a Christian pastor was usually sufficient cause for people to believe that God would care for them—even when they felt disillusioned themselves. They leaned on the faith I represent. And before long, most of them reported that God had given them the strength and reassurance they needed. Such people are open to discover God's care.

Not so my friend. He and I hold different frameworks. Although we are good friends, within his framework my pastoral status has little authority. He is not able to believe God cares just because I do. Nor is he able to believe God cares because the church says so. He does his own believing through the only framework he trusts—his own. Looking at the world through that framework he has not seen evidence that convinces him God actively cares about what happens in his life. As a matter of fact, he tells me each day he sees more evidence that God is either powerless or not directly concerned about individuals. He is neither a cynical nor disillusioned person. He says he had no illusions to begin with; he has always believed he has to take care of himself. And he has.

Christians from Without

How different my friend is from those among whom most clergy serve. Few of the Strivers among whom I ministered during the years after World War II resemble my friend whose wife was killed. To be sure, the contingencies of life challenged their faith. But most often their struggles and responses were quite different from those of my more contemporary friend.

Faced with the disruptive effects of social change, I watched many Strivers, dislocated from their communities and neighborhoods, struggle to recover the roots that had always supported their faith and life. Like Stewart and Stella, whose move to St. Louis separated them spatially from the close community that had always been there to reaffirm their framework, they sought to regain their roots in the old order by joining a church in the place to which they moved. In that post-World War II world of radical social change the church, with its traditional, rural-flavored liturgy of worship and group life, reassured them that the old plausibility structure was still somehow intact. Bolstered by familiar hymns, church suppers, and Sunday school picnics, singing and eating in new buildings made to look old, for years Strivers were able to maintain faith in their reflective frameworks.

Not so Challengers and Calculators. Like my grief-stricken friend, those who have been socialized after the prime time of the Strivers usually lack a nostalgic framework that includes an integrated world. They cannot join a new congregation in order to secure their belief in the church's pervasive involvement with all of life, and, by implication, God's presence in all of life, because they never had such a sense to begin with. Few of them have experienced rootedness in a church-dominated society, like many Strivers recall.

Those roots through the church were taken for granted by most Strivers. During the prime-time years of the Strivers I seldom heard anyone ask, "Are you a Christian?" Within Striver culture the question "Are you a Christian?" usually feels unnecessary, even foolish. A typical response is something like "Why, of course I am—and an American too!"

The Strivers' framework assumes a basic belonging. Among Strivers the more appropriate question is "Are you a Presbyterian or a United Methodist or a Roman Catholic?" For Strivers, the key differentiation is the way an individual identifies herself or himself *within* the church culture, not whether she or he belongs. As a pastor with this cohort and those that preceded them I have often been struck by the fact that those who are not active in any church are usually clear about the church they stay away from. A Jew, although obviously not a Christian in terms of belief, still feels like someone who belongs.[1]

The core act of believing, for Strivers, is belonging, as I discovered quite forcefully while a pastor during the early sixties. To the dismay of their traditional Striver parents, the members of one of my confirmation classes reflected the new age that was then dawning. The Sunday evening after Easter this group of fourteen- and fifteen-year-olds told me they had decided they did *not* want to join the church after all. Why? Because after several weeks of studying what Christians traditionally have believed, they found themselves unable to accept various key points of Christian doctrine. Without realizing the implications of my decision, I told them I agreed that they should not join the church if they did not believe key tenets of the Christian faith.

The news of my "permissiveness" traveled fast. The church board meeting the following Tuesday evening was heated. One of the church elders, the father of one of the young people in the confirmation class, was most outspoken. Why had I gone along with the young people, he wanted to know. "Because they don't believe in God the way Christians do," I replied. "So what," he responded, "the important thing is for them to join the church. They can figure out what they believe later."

For an hour the church board and I went round and round: they insisting that belonging can precede believing, I insisting that belonging to church only makes sense if one is a Christian in terms of belief. We were facing an issue that none of us had faced before. And that night none of us appreciated the fundamental nature of the issue: those young people, taking courage from their cohort, were challenging a fundamental aspect of the Striver framework.

Regardless of what particular individuals may or may not believe, the church is an essential ingredient in the Striver framework. Many Strivers are dependent believers. In the board meeting that night we all knew that people had doubted before; most of us had had some doubts ourselves. But we had learned to subordinate our doubts to the norm of belonging and join up. Where we could not believe, we trusted the church to do our believing. That's what our framework called for. And it worked so long as we could believe the Striver framework approximated reality. But once we became aware that the social structure on which that framework rested was undermined by social change, so was the basis for our faith. I now know that many of those who argued with me that night were frightened; if the young people were right, their faith was in trouble as well.

Challenger and Calculator frameworks do not encourage such dependent believing. As a matter of fact, they encourage the opposite. Charlene and Chuck leave the church because they have substantive theological and ethical disagreements with the church, not because they don't like the minister, or someone criticizes the way they have organized the Sunday school or finance committee. They leave because their theological and ethical perspectives disagree with what they see as the church's perspective.

Challengers assume they have both the right and the responsibility to do their own believing. Chuck tries a variety of approaches, in the end receiving more help from a Zen master than he had from his church. His parents, like Carl's, misunderstand his entire approach and the way both his needs and his framework differ from theirs. To them he seems dangerously disloyal to the church, in much the same way that his CO status during the war seemed disloyal to the nation.

Quite unlike the Strivers, most of those socialized since the mid-1960s look on Christian believing as one of a number of faith options. Many, like Chuck, have explored alternative ways of believing. Others, like Carolyn, have not been moved to explore personally any faith option—even those who, like my grief-stricken friend, have faced significant adversity.

Many Calculators, like Carl and Calvin and Carrie, choose a congregation that reflects what they believe in and that supports and nurtures their faith. The congregation may appear to concur with many beliefs and lifeways Strivers also can affirm, but the way the Calvins and Carries enter is more like conversion than simply acceptance. They join with conviction. They choose a church that supports beliefs that match their own. They reverse the Strivers' usual pattern: they believe first and then they may belong.

Those of us who have been socialized more recently, within a segmented, pluralistic culture, have not internalized the old Striver framework. Few of us hold church-based perspectives on reality that we trust are accurate—even where, as individuals, we cannot see how they might be. Few of us become believers within an integrated, church-world, social context anymore, by acculturation, because so much of what composes our culture is separated from the church's direct influence. Nor do we think we have to believe God is effectively present when we cannot see that God is effectively present. Like my grief-stricken friend, we feel as free to admit what we do not believe as former cohorts felt constrained to adhere to what they were supposed to believe. And the authority of a church or a pastor is no longer sufficient to give credibility to the Christian perspective. Most of us now trust our own perception as much as or more than we do the church.

Ways to Christian Faith

A few years ago I made a retreat with a group that included a Trappist retreat master. During the days of quiet together we became good friends. One afternoon, while we were sharing our concern for helping people grow in faith, he described how he sometimes responds to young adults who come to him for spiritual guidance.

Many begin, he said, by telling him of their previous attempts to find a sense of fulfillment. Often their stories conclude with statements of frustration, like: "Father, I have been on a quest for years. In my previous attempts to find personal fulfillment I have given myself to causes of social justice; I have tried encounter groups; I have tried meditation; I have even tried various drugs. While each of these experiences seemed promising in the beginning, nothing I have tried has given me ultimate satisfaction. I admire the great sense of peace that many monks seem to show. Have you anything to suggest that might help me?"

The retreat master told me his intuition sometimes leads him to respond to such inquirers by saying: "Perhaps I do. Would you be willing to try an experiment. For the next month sit quietly and meditate for fifteen minutes of each day. Occasionally repeat the word, 'Jesus' to yourself, softly. If you notice anything significant during your meditation, come back at the end of the month and tell me about it."

At the end of a month about half of the young people return. Most of them describe a sense of "something" or "someone" who, they say, is trying to reach them. The retreat master then gives each of these young people a copy of the Gospel of John. "I tell them to read it through twice, reading only one chapter each day. And I ask them to come back and share with me what they perceive."

"Most of those who read through the Gospel return at the end of a second month to tell me, 'Now I know who is trying to reach out to me.' "

My Trappist friend then looked straight at me and said, "You and I know that God is alive and active in this world. Because that is so, we are open to encounters with God ourselves. We should also feel free to suggest to others how they may discover the living God as well."

I am impressed with this retreat master's cultural and theological perceptiveness. From a theological perspective, I believe we do not need to find God, but to perceive God who is seeking us. God has already initiated the encounter. Such a belief is reinforced repeatedly in my experience and is a cardinal perspective within my framework.

The "Jesus prayer" the retreat master suggests to Challenger young adults has centuries-old roots within the Christian mystical tradition. For hundreds of years Christians have prayed it to help them focus their meditation. But the Jesus prayer also resembles some of the meditative techniques that are popular among Challengers, which may be why serious inquirers within this generation find that praying it helps them discover the reality of God. The retreat master's wisdom is displayed in his ability to draw on a reliable tradition in such a way that it speaks of possible Christian faith within the framework of those who are still outsiders to that faith.

Striver Christians with whom I share the approach my Trappist friend follows are usually impressed because the Challenger young people find faith. But they seldom appreciate how his approach addresses the unique needs of Challengers. Strivers in their prime time struggled to hang on to their faith when they were pulled away from their roots. When they were forced to move from place to place by their work, for example, Strivers sought a church in each new place to keep their roots.

Challengers and Calculators often face a more radical dilemma than Strivers did during those postwar years; many in these later cohorts lack a sense of rootedness in the cosmos itself. They are not simply temporarily uprooted from their home community or neighborhood. They have been socialized within a segmented world. In their experience all institutions, including the church, do not provide evidence of a stable, reliable order of creation under the providence of God. Strivers' perceptions of the abidiing sanctity of nation and marriage and church and God seem to many members of succeeding cohorts to be naive, and perhaps even based in self-deception. Challengers and Calculators have seen too many questionable examples of marriage and church to believe in the basic sanctity of what each is supposed to represent. And they have felt free to see them. Their frameworks do not encourage them to see marriages and governments and churches through rose-colored glasses.

Nor is the presence of a minister or involvement in church sufficient to reassure their faith. For those who come after the time of the Strivers the problem is not simply "Where can I fit in again?" but "Does any overarching, integrating order under God exist? Is there any secure, benevolent order to fit into?" For them the basic problem is not recovering a sense that they belong, but believing in the first place.

This emergent need helps to explain why spiritual formation has become more and more a focus of concern today. If people have to do their own believing, to make their own individual way to faith, then many will need help to do so. Although Strivers may see spiritual guidance to be about as necessary as Parent Effectiveness Training, those from other cohorts, who do not share their cultural assurance, often benefit from both. The stable social order that includes widely accepted patterns on which both parents and believers can depend no longer exists. People no longer know what it means to be parents or believers simply by recalling where they belong.

The idea of faith "development" is strange to many church members for another reason. Those of us who have long experience with the church are accustomed to viewing believing normatively rather than developmentally. Like the Striver parents of those young people in my rebellious confirmation class, we see the appropriate goal as deciding to fit in and believe what is "right." Ministers are supposed to know what is right and teach that to others. Within such a framework believing is like being moral.

The developmental approach, by contrast, envisions believing more in terms of a process or a journey. It focuses on identifying the different ways or styles or stages that people follow as they become believers. One of the more helpful writers in the area of Christian nurture today is John Westerhoff. Westerhoff describes four "styles" of faith that people exhibit as they make their way to believing: experienced faith, affiliative faith, searching faith, and owned faith.[2] He sees the nurturing task of the church (which I think he describes superbly) as one of helping people to move appropriately through the styles.

In Westerhoff's view, each of us begins our faith journey with whatever faith we come to during early years at home and perhaps in the church. If we can affirm that basic faith and decide we want to belong to the community that has nurtured us, we move into the next style, or affiliative faith. Then in the process of maturing, especially as we engage the wider world beyond our own community and culture, we may enter a questioning phase. This style of faith is a time when we examine our own beliefs critically, as well as the beliefs that have been given to us and perhaps the beliefs of others who are different from our own faith community. Finally, if we find the resources needed to address our questions, we may move on to owned faith, a mature style of believing, when faith is based on clear personal convictions.

Since reading Westerhoff's book I have often noted that members of different cohorts tend to function more easily within certain of the styles of faith he describes. Most Strivers, for example, begin with experienced faith and move on quite naturally from that given faith to affiliative faith. They see the movement from experienced faith to affiliative faith as a normal part of growing up. It is a matter of taking one's place within the faith community, the church. And many Strivers think that to belong and know that one belongs is faith enough.

Such a view explains why the questioning members of my confirmation class were such a puzzle and perhaps a threat to their parents. Their questioning and doubts about "the faith" and their unwillingness to fit in seemed unnatural, even downright dangerous, to their Striver parents.

But theirs was not simply a case of adolescent rebellion, as their parents wanted me to believe. Many of the adolescents did finally "come around" and join the church on Pentecost, but most of them did not find a way spiritually to belong. In fact, some have never decided to belong. They were early defectors from church, forerunners of the several million Challengers who left the church as young people (which was not unusual) and who have not returned (which is unusual), much to the consternation of their Striver parents and other Striver church members.

In those early years most of us did not realize how different the approach many Challengers take to believing is from the styles of believing with which we were familiar. Questioning is normal and not threatening for Challengers. It is natural for them in the same way that looking for a way to fit in is natural for Strivers.

In my work as a church planner I have often noticed that members of different cohorts are best able to meet their needs for faith development within group configurations that support their typical approaches to believing. In Figure 6:1 I have diagrammed the group patterns within which I have observed members of each cohort are best able to explore believing. (In each diagram "L" stands for leader and "M" for member of the group or congregation.)

Within Strivers' framework, faith is usually viewed as a tradition that is passed from generation to generation. Leaders are respected guardians of that tradition: the elders who teach the younger. The unit is more basic than the individual. Individuals shape their faith according to traditions accepted by their family and faith community. Each one becomes a full believer by assenting to the traditional, given faith. Such movement into full believing is often marked by a rite of passage, like confirmation, in which an individual declares publicly that he or she affirms the faith given. Within such a style of faith development each person gains the needed resources for believing largely by listening.

This typical Striver approach to believing assumes a continuing, stable order that integrates social and theological realities. By the prime time of the Challengers such an order has disintegrated, and as we have seen in this book, most people socialized in the new cohorts doubt that it ever existed. As a result, only a few persons acculturated during the past two decades believe they can find a satisfactory faith by fitting into a given tradition. Few see any given tradition as currently reliable. Most feel that they are on their own and must deal with their own questions with the resources available in their own time. Reliable suggestions for believing are just as likely—probably more likely—to come from contemporaries as they are to come from the elders. Change has undermined much of the authority of tradition. Although the elders may still be authorities on the tradition, they do not have an authoritative experience of the new world in which members of the new cohort have to live out the traditional faith. The suggestions they make about

Figure 6:1 Typical Cohort Learning Patterns

Strivers Listen

L

M M M M M M M M M
M M M M M M M M M
M M M M M M M M M
M M M M M M M M M
M M M M M M M M M

Challengers Question

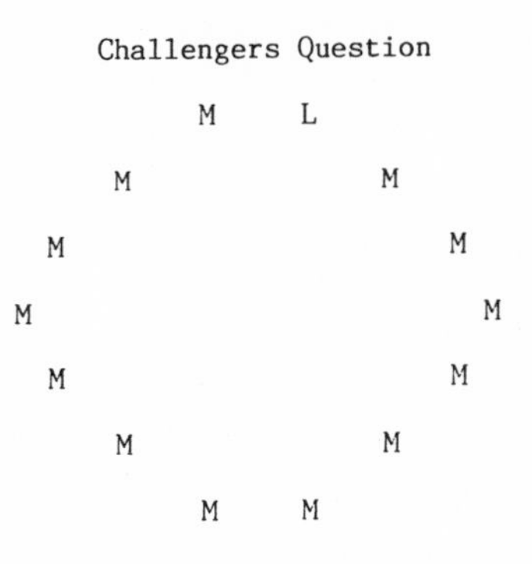

Calculators Scrutinize

L

M M

M M

M M

M M

believing often seem to Challengers to reflect and assume a world that no longer exists.

When Challengers approach the church they need the opportunity to state *their* questions. The questions many congregations are prepared to answer reflect Strivers' perception of the way people "should" come to faith. They seldom address Challengers' agendas. In fact, given the great variety of perspectives within Challenger culture, it often takes particular Challengers some time to clarify the dilemmas that need to be addressed if they are to make their way to faith.

The leader who is sensitive to Challengers will spend as much time, if not more, listening as talking. He or she will need to be as skilled in helping them share relevant insights with one another as he or she is in putting them all in touch with the tradition. The leader will need to be able to sense what avenues may lead individual group members to believing and encourage each to explore those that are appropriate. He or she will probably learn as much from the group as the group learns from him or her. Challengers' natural approach to faith is through questioning.

Calculators tend to be both more pragmatic and cautious in their approach to faith than do Challengers. They are not as likely to believe that tradition has nothing to offer them. But unlike Strivers, they do not feel obligated to fit into the tradition within which they were raised. Among Calculators, given faith is more respected than it is among Challengers, but it is not determinative, as it often is among Strivers.

Many Calculators, like Challengers, have not been socialized in any faith tradition. They feel as free to choose the way they will believe as Challengers do but are not as likely to consider radical approaches to believing. Calculators scrutinize. They expect to learn from one another, but they value a leader who knows the consequences of following various options. They don't feel the freedom to experiment that Challengers do (did). They want a faith that will anchor them solidly in an indestructible reality. They question but are usually more intentional and clearer about what they are seeking than Challengers are.

Challengers and Calculators who become Christians tend to do so as adults, often after an extended period of questioning. They are much less likely to be developmental Christians, who take on faith as part of growing up. Christian believing for Challengers and Calculators is usually based in faith they have chosen.

Members of each cohort are not always able to appreciate the way members of another approach believe. In fact, sometimes when members of one cohort dominate a congregation, they shape its life to meet their own needs, to the exclusion of others. Those Striver parents whose Challenger children in my confirmation class decided not to join the church understandably looked on their children's rebelliousness as an adolescent phenomenon. Twenty years ago few of us could see the unique needs of Challengers. Yet I still see countless Striver-dominated congregations that refuse to recognize questioning faith as a legitimate avenue people should take to faith. Challengers and Calculators, with their need to question, find it difficult to be nurtured in such congregations.

I also have been in settings where Challengers are equally unaware or intolerant. Some Challengers, for example, want to make all worship services informal. Such a narrow perspective overlooks the need of many Strivers for a structured, predictable, orderly worship experience. As one exasperated Striver complained, after repeated services that began with informal "sharings of the failings we have experienced during the past week," "Couldn't we begin just one service with something like, 'Almighty God, unto whom all hearts are open . . .?' "

Members of each cohort are tempted to make norms out of the style of believing that works best for them, or that represents the way they came to faith. Thus, Strivers affirm affiliative faith as all that is necessary; while Challengers think believers are not solid unless they have passed through times of deep questioning. Calculators, in their concern to find a solid place to anchor in what they especially perceive as a precarious and unstable world, are tempted to come to premature closure and own a faith that is simplistic. Calculators who choose such a course often associate with congregations that offer them protection but that require rigid believing in return. Such Calculators then look on Challengers who question and Strivers who hold to a less rigid tradition as lacking in real faith.

I think congregations today need to recognize the legitimacy of a variety of ways to believe. Caring churches will provide varied resources and settings, so that those who turn to them may find the support they need to continue their own faith journeys. And sensitive leaders will, like my Trappist friend, help them discover how God is already at work at their lives.

Sharing Faith

As I have sought to encourage Christian faith among those who have grown into adulthood during the past two decades, I have become more and more troubled by the church's accepted characterization of Christian outreach as "mission." A year ago, while helping leaders of a local church clarify the church's opportunities for outreach, I interviewed a woman who had recently become active in that congregation. Her return to the church after an absence of nearly twenty years was helped considerably by the ministry of the perceptive, caring young woman who is her pastor. She described how her pastor's patient listening had enabled her to work through some important questions that for years had alienated her from Christians.

The woman then went on to talk about her husband, who is neither a Christian nor a church member. She told me he still has many of the questions she once had.

"Suppose this congregation, where you have found so much help, were to make a sincere effort to reach out to your husband. Would you welcome that?" I asked.

"No," she replied, "I would run the other way as fast as I could."

"Why?" I asked, quite surprised at her response.

"Because," she said, "he is not ready. And he might identify me with the church's attempt to manipulate him."

It took several minutes to put her at ease again. She then went on to recount oppressive experiences each of them had had with churches during their growing-up years. I assured her this congregation and pastor (whom I know well) would be more patient and sensitive.

This woman and her husband are examples of people who I feel have been abused by the "mission" approach to evangelism. I doubt that such an understanding of outreach, with its accompanying military images of Christians as Christ's army, bent on conquering the world in Christ's name, was ever an appropriate representation of the Christian faith. It is certainly an inappropriate, if not harmful, approach today.[3]

A mission understanding of outreach usually envisions the church as central and powerful, in a position to dominate—which it clearly is not today. It also assumes that Christians are right and others are wrong, and therefore deserve to be conquered or, to use mission terminology, "converted." Christians who operate in such a mode come across more as ecclesiastical imperialists than as persons concerned to help others believe. And those who have suffered under their abuse will rightly "run the other way"—to use the words of the woman I interviewed.

My own understanding of Christian faith and my attempts to help others with their believing lead me to conclude that "sharing" is a more appropriate understanding of outreach than is mission. Sharing means offering what we have or have discovered to others. It requires sensitivity and respect. We need to consider how the others currently approach believing, what has happened to them at the hands of other Christians, whether this is the appropriate time to share with them, and whether we or some other Christian can be most helpful to them. We need to be as aware of the frameworks of those with whom we seek to share as we are of our own. Sharing is different from forcing or manipulating. It is more like giving than conquering.

Living by Grace

Encouraging others to live as Christians also involves as much sensitivity to their needs and situations as to our own. In a complex world such as ours, ethical commitments will necessarily be as varied as ways to faith. Not long ago I shared with someone the story of the physicist's decision to quit his job when he became aware that his efforts to help design power plants for submarines were contributing to instruments of death.

"Does he pay all of his taxes?" this new person wanted to know.

"I don't know," I responded.

"Well, I think if he really is concerned not to contribute to instruments of death, then he should withhold the portion of his federal income taxes that support the defense budget."

The new person then went on to explain that he and his wife are tax protesters. Each year they withhold a portion of their taxes equal to the proportion of the federal budget that goes to the Defense Department. They report all their income and include a letter with their tax return explaining why their ethical commitment prevents them from paying the full amount of taxes due.

"Eventually they catch up with you," he explained, "and take the money out of your bank account—plus interest. But my wife and I feel we have kept our integrity by not giving it voluntarily."

What must we do to live faithfully today? I doubt there is one set of rules that will adequately encompass the great variety of life situations that I believe may call for different responses from each of us.

To return to our example, the message of the sixth commandment is clear: "You shall not kill." What it means to obey that commandment in circumstances where our individual action is not constrained by other forces is not difficult to define: we should not kill.

But so much of our living is carried on in segments where we do not exercise complete control. Our actions are constrained by those of others. How do we respond under such conditions? Is it wrong to kill in a time of war, perhaps by piloting a ship or airplane from which someone else launches the actual instruments of killing? Does our Christian faith forbid us to serve, as some of us believe, as members of our country's armed forces? Is it wrong to support in any way any organization or system that contributes to killing? At what point is it right to draw the line? Different Christians come to different conclusions on the basis of their different frameworks and commitments.

Ours is no world for moralists. In a complex world, where we seldom exercise complete control over our lives, moralists, with their simplistic assumption that ethical decisions nearly always involve a clear right and a clear wrong, may encourage us to be dishonest either about ourselves or about the nature of the world in which we live or both.

Often the most ethical response is to accept openly the painful compromises necessary to stay within a difficult segment and seek to check whatever abuse we can. Such was the costly and faithful decision Susan (chapter 4) made when she determined to remain within the agency after she uncovered financial impropriety. And those within her local congregation, with whom she shared her dilemma, supported her in that decision—even those who disagreed with her.

Moralists seldom accept the segmented nature of our society. They encourage us to withdraw from the world of ambiguities as much as possible, in order to protect ourselves from compromises. But the end result of such pulling away may be to eliminate whatever good influence we might have had in the segments from which we have withdrawn. All of us face ethical decisions within segments where we do not have complete control over the consequences of our actions. As citizens, young people have to decide whether they will or will not seek to register as conscientious objectors to war. Others among us must decide whether to give up lucrative positions when we become aware that our work contributes to the development of instruments of killing. And all of us must decide whether to pay all of our taxes.

Such decisions are painful, but real. We will often find ourselves coming to different conclusions about what is right to do where there is no obvious, absolute right way to act. In such circumstances the awareness that we live faithfully by grace, not by being good, is indispensable. Sin is as much a condition as it is an option. We may be able to avoid particular sins, but not sin.

To think we can or should be able to escape sin may encourage us to adopt narrow, categorical moral positions that meet our own needs. We become self-righteous and intolerant. We then direct attention away from our own failings and focus on certain sins that are particularly repulsive to us.

Abortion, for example, is identified currently by many Christians as always wrong. Yet a woman who seeks an abortion is certainly not categorically less ethical or godly than a man who kills enemies in a time of war.

An act of killing in war is no easier to justify than abortion. Choosing sins on which to concentrate our attention may blind us to the greater reality of sin in ourselves as well as in the world.

All of us need to be challenged as well as supported. Ethical decisions are no more subject to normative criteria than ways to faith. Exposing ourselves only to those who see the world from our perspective increases the possibility of self-deception. History abounds with examples of those who adopted a narrow, categorical ethical perspective and then abused others in the name of God—even recent history. Congregations need to be open to a variety of ethical perspectives as well as a variety of faith perspectives. The faithful congregation will be a place of challenge as well as a place of comfort.

There is much more I could say about strategies that churches can use to nurture Christian faith and support faithful living today. As I indicated at the beginning of this chapter, in a subsequent book I plan to spell out some suggestions in detail. I wrote this present book first because it provides a necessary foundation for the one that follows.

In this book I have sought to describe the overall frameworks through which people in our present society approach believing and living. The framework through which each of us perceives the world fundamentally shapes the way each of us believes and lives. As a Christian, I believe God can come to us and call us to faithful living through that framework. Whether we view the world as Strivers, Challengers, or Calculators, or through some other framework, God can encourage us to faith and faithful living through the unique perspectives that shape our individual approaches to believing. By God's grace all our frameworks of believing can become frameworks of faith.

Notes

Chapter 1 Perspectives

1. I am using "seeing" and "looking" here generically, as the equivalents of what we perceive and the way we have decided what we will perceive.
2. See especially William James, *The Principles of Psychology* (Cambridge, MA: Harvard University Press, 1981), ch. 21; the writings of G.H. Mead; Alfred Schutz, *Collected Papers,* ed. Maurice Natanson (The Hague: Martinus Nijhoff, 1962), esp. pt. 3; Jean Piaget, *The Construction of Reality in the Child* (New York: Ballantine Books, 1954); Erving Goffman, *The Presentation of Self in Everyday Life* (Garden City, NY: Doubleday, 1959); Robert Wuthnow, *The Consciousness Reformation* (Berkeley: University of California Press, 1976), ch. 2; Walter Lippmann, *Public Opinion* (New York: Macmillan, 1922).
3. "That's Why Darkies Were Born." Copyright 1931 by De Sylva, Brown, and Henderson, Inc., NY.
4. Lesslie Newbigin, *The Other Side of 1984* (Geneva: World Council of Churches, 1983), pp. 9–10.
5. Michael Polanyi, *Personal Knowledge* (Chicago: University of Chicago Press, 1958), ch. 9.
6. Ibid., pp. 288–89.
7. For a description of this congregation see Elizabeth O'Connor, *Call to Commitment* (New York: Harper & Row, 1963).
8. Adlai Stevenson, *Putting First Things First—A Democratic View* (New York: Random House, 1960), pp. 27ff.
9. See Gerald J. Jud, Edgar W. Mills Jr., Genevieve Walters Burch, *Ex-Pastors* (New York: The Pilgrim Press, 1970).
10. Jeffrey Hadden, *The Gathering Storm in the Churches* (Garden City, NY: Doubleday, 1969).
11. John Baskin, "The Preacher and the Plumber's Son," *Country Journal* 12, no. 4 (April 1985):59–60.
12. For an early description of this process see C. Wright Mills, *The Power Elite* (New York: Oxford University Press, 1956).
13. Daniel Yankelovich, *New Rules* (New York: Random House, 1981).
14. Alvin Toffler, *Future Shock* (New York: Random House, 1970).

Chapter 2 Living in Spaces

1. See Richard Lingeman, *Small Town America* (New York: G.P. Putnam's Sons, 1980).
2. See James Oliver Robinson, *American Myth, American Reality* (New York: Hill & Wang, 1980), esp. pp. 215–28.
3. Although Alvin Toffler's *Future Shock* (New York: Random House, 1970) is more familiar to many of us, an excellent study, completed when the change was still new to people's experience, is Robert Presthus, *The Organizational Society* (New York: Alfred A. Knopf, 1962).
4. William Goodwin, "Approaching Rural Ministry" (Washington, DC: Glenmary Research Center, n.d.), mimeo. See also Roland L. Warren, *The Community in America* (New York: Rand McNally, 1974).
5. *Central Maine Morning Sentinel,* August 15, 1985, p. 1.
6. William H. Whyte, "The Wife Problem." Reprinted in *Fortune* Anniversary Issue, February 11, 1980, p. 129. I recently talked with a young man employed by the same company. He reported that membership in the country club is still available to employees, although the fee is higher; it now costs each family $5 per year.
7. See Wade Clark Roof, *Community and Commitment* (New York: Elsevier, 1978). See also Robert K. Merton, *Social Theory and Social Structure* (New York: The Free Press, 1968), ch. 11; also Robert N. Bellah, Richard Madsen, William M. Sullivan, Ann Swidler, and Steven M. Tipton, *Habits of the Heart* (Berkeley: University of California Press, 1985).
8. See Erving Goffman, *The Presentation of the Self in Everyday Life* (Garden City, NY: Doubleday, 1959).
9. Perhaps the best-known book is Nena O'Neill and George O'Neill's *Open Marriage* (New York: Evans, 1972). James Ramsey's *Intimate Friendships* (Englewood Cliffs, NJ: Prentice-Hall, 1976) offers an excellent description of the attitudes at the height of the approach's popularity. Daniel Yankelovich describes those who currently hold to open marriage in *New Rules* (New York: Random House, 1981).
10. Calvin L. Beale, "The Revival of Population Growth in Nonmetropolitan America," U.S. Department of Agriculture Economic Research Service Bulletin ERS-605. See also Beale's article, "Renewed Growth in Rural Communities," *The Futurist* 9, no. 4 (August 1975):196–202. See also Lingeman, *Small Town America,* ch. 10.
11. Willis N. Ellis, "The New Ruralism: The Post-Industrial Age Is Upon Us," *The Futurist* 9, no. 4 (August 1975):204.
12. From *Identity and Anxiety: Survival of the Person in Mass Society,* ed. Maurice R. Stein, Arthur J. Vidich, and David Manning White. (Glencoe, IL: The Free Press, 1960), pp. 183–84. Copyright © 1960 by The Free Press, a Corporation. Used by permission of Macmillan Publishing Company.

Chapter 3 Living Through Our Own Times

1. Margaret Mead, *Culture and Commitment* (Garden City, NY: Natural History Press/Doubleday, 1970), p. 63.
2. Karl Mannheim, "The Problem of Generations," ch. 7, in his collected *Essays on the Sociology of Knowledge,* ed. Paul Kecskemeti (London: Routledge & Kegan Paul, 1952), p. 303. Mannheim's essay contains the most helpful description of cohort formation. Those familiar with his work will recognize my indebtedness to him.
3. Ibid., p. 300. Mannheim suggests age twenty-five as the point at which language (and, by inference, the socialization process we are describing) is fixed. That seems too old to me; age twenty-two or twenty-three seems more likely.
4. Russell Baker, *Growing Up* (New York: Condon & Weed, 1982), pp. 158–59.
5. See Charles Hamm, *Yesterdays, Popular Song in America* (New York: W.W. Norton, 1979).
6. See Daniel Yankelovich, *New Rules* (New York: Random House, 1981), esp. pt. 3.
7. See the 1985 study conducted by Frank S. Levy and Richard C. Michel for the Joint Economic Committee of the U.S. Congress; Landon Y. Jones, *Great Expectations: America and the Baby Boom Generation* (New York: Coward, McCann & Geoghegan, 1980), esp. pt. 4; Yankelovich, *New Rules.*
8. The prime shaping years, and, as a consequence, the present functioning of early and late baby boomers, are so different that to treat them as a single cohort is a mistake.
9. See "The Year of the Yuppie," *Newsweek,* December 31, 1984, pp. 14ff.
10. Currently, there are several resources available that describe this scaling down in some detail, including Jones, *Great Expectations;* Yankelovich, *New Rules;* and "The Economic Future of the Baby Boom," a report to the Joint Economic Committee of the U.S. Congress, by Frank S. Levy and Richard C. Michel of the Urban Institute at the University of Maryland (released December 5, 1985).
11. David Nyhan, "Today's Campus Is No Place for Do-gooders," *Central Maine Morning Sentinel,* February 10, 1986, p. 12. For a picture of the way in which this pattern continues, see Gwen Kinkead, "On a Fast Track to the Good Life—Today's Twenty-five-year-old Business Beginners Know What They Want and Are Uninhibited About Demanding It," *Fortune,* April 7, 1980, pp. 74–84.
12. Using a cohort approach, someone better equipped than I needs to examine how social change has affected the patterns of living and believing of minority persons.
13. Arnold Mitchell, *The Nine American Lifestyles* (New York: Macmillan, 1983), p. 63.

Chapter 4 Churches Caught in Space and Time

1. *The Evanston Report, The Second Assembly of the World Council of Churches, 1954* (London: SCM Press, 1954), p. 168. Interestingly, I

saw these same words quoted only one month ago in a brochure describing a conference on lay ministry to be held at a nearby seminary.

2. See Douglas Alan Walrath, "The Congregations of the Synod of Albany," a report in several parts, published by the Synod of Albany, Reformed Church in America, 1970–1984.
3. See *Understanding Church Growth and Decline, 1950–78*, ed. Dean Hoge and David Roozen (New York: The Pilgrim Press, 1979), esp. ch. 11 by Ruth T. Doyle and Sheila M. Kelly, "Comparison of Trends in Ten Denominations: 1950–75." Although lower birthrates and higher median ages of members tend to be associated with denominations that report the greatest losses, status factors with attendant life-style differences are a significant contributor.
4. Wade Clark Roof, *Community and Commitment* (New York: Elsevier, 1978).
5. Robert K. Merton, *Social Theory and Social Structure* (enlarged ed.; New York: The Free Press, 1968).
6. Roof, *Community and Commitment,* p. 81.
7. John A.T. Robinson, *Honest to God* (Philadelphia: Westminster Press, 1963); Joseph Fletcher, *Situation Ethics* (Philadelphia: Westminster Press, 1966; Fletcher's article "The New Look in Christian Ethics" appeared in the *Harvard Divinity Bulletin,* October 1959, pp. 7–18.
8. Robinson, *Honest to God,* chs. 1–3.
9. Ibid., p. 110.
10. Fletcher, "The New Look," p. 10; quoted by Robinson, *Honest to God,* p. 116.
11. Ibid.
12. See ch. 2.
13. An excellent summary of the origins of this movement is Donald M. Scott, *From Office to Profession: The New England Ministry, 1750–1850* (Philadelphia: University of Pennsylvania Press, 1978).
14. Bruce S. Cooper, of Fordham University, and James S. Catterall, of UCLA, quoted in the *Central Maine Morning Sentinel,* September 3, 1985, p. 1.
15. Dean Kelley, *Why Conservative Churches Are Growing* (New York: Harper & Row, 1972).
16. James Oliver Robinson, *American Myth, American Reality* (New York: Hill & Wang, 1980), pp. 218ff.
17. Peter Schrag, *The End of the American Future* (New York: Simon and Schuster, 1973), p. 100; quoted in Robinson, *American Myth,* p. 227.
18. Ibid.
19. See Thomas J.J. Altizer and William Hamilton, *Radical Theology and the Death of God* (Indianapolis: Bobbs-Merrill, 1966), which collects the short articles that appeared in various publications.
20. In the paragraphs that follow, my indebtedness to Peter Berger and Thomas Luckmann will become increasingly apparent. See their *The Social Construction of Reality* (Garden City, NY: Doubleday, Anchor

Books, 1967); also Berger's *The Sacred Canopy* (Garden City, NY: Doubleday, Anchor Books, 1969); Luckmann's *The Invisible Religion, The Problem of Religion in Modern Society* (New York: Macmillan, 1967); and Peter Berger, Brigitte Berger, and Hansfried Kellner, *The Homeless Mind, Modernization and Consciousness* (New York: Vintage Books, 1974).

21. Louis Dupres, "Spiritual Life in a Secular Age," in *Religion and America, Spiritual Life in a Secular Age,* ed. Mary Douglas and Steven Tipton. (Boston: Beacon Press, 1982, 1983), p. 6. Italics in the original.
22. Berger, *Sacred Canopy,* p. 45.
23. See Luckmann, *Invisible Religion,* p. 89.

Chapter 5 Believing Through Our Own Times

1. *Newsweek,* November 21, 1983, p. 66.
2. Marcia Yudkin, "When Kids Think the Unthinkable," *Psychology Today* 18, no. 4 (April 1984):19.
3. Ibid., p. 20.
4. Marie Winn, *Children Without Childhood* (New York: Pantheon Books, 1983); see also her "What Became of Childhood Innocence?" *The New York Times Magazine,* January 25, 1981, pp. 14ff.
5. *Newsweek* 101, no. 10 (March 7, 1983):32.
6. Daniel Yankelovich, in *New Rules* (New York: Random House, 1981) has a clear description of Challengers' feeling they ought to do what they want to do. See esp. chs. 5–8.
7. Alexis de Tocqueville, quoted by Martin Marty in *A Nation of Behavers* (Chicago: University of Chicago Press, 1976), p. 201.

Chapter 6 Nurturing Christian Faith

1. See Will Herberg's classic study of this phenomenon, *Protestant-Catholic-Jew* (Garden City, NY: Doubleday, Anchor Books, 1960).
2. John Westerhoff, *Will Our Children Have Faith?* (New York: Seabury Press, 1976), see esp. ch. 4. See also James Fowler, *Stages of Faith* (San Francisco: Harper & Row, 1981).
3. My observations here are not intended to criticize individual missionaries, many of whom are among the finest Christians I know.

DIFFERENT CONCLUSIONS 90
BELIEVING KEY TENETS 91